50
YEARS
OF
ALOHA

50 YEARS OF ALOHA

The Story of Aloha Airlines

By Bill Wood

Published by Aloha Airlines, Incorporated
P.O. Box 30028
Honolulu, Hawaii 96820
Copyright © 1996 by Bill Wood
Book Design by Turner & de Vries, Ltd.

Bill Wood.
50 Years of Aloha, The Story of Aloha Airlines /
Bill Wood — 1st ed.
Includes index
Library of Congress Catalog Card Number: 96-85497

ISBN 0-9652781-0-7
First Edition 1996
Printed in Singapore

Dedication

*G*lenn Zander and the other chief executives who have led Aloha Airlines toward its next half-century unanimously credit one man for giving the company the foresight and commitment that have positioned it so well for whatever the future may bring. That man is Dr. Hung Wo Ching, the wiry, crew-cut businessman with the starched collar and jaunty bow tie who was so much a part of Aloha's long history and was its guiding force through its greatest trials.

Hung Wo Ching was a giant in the modern history of Hawaii, a pioneer who contributed to the sweeping economic, social and political changes that transformed these islands from the languid, feudal society of yesteryear to the modern, dynamic blend of East and West that they are today. That all this happened in the adult lifetime of one man is a powerful reminder of how far Hawaii has come in so short a time. And that one man played so large a role in that progress is high tribute to his vision and determination.

Dr. Hung Wo Ching
1912 - 1996

There were many instances in which Dr. Ching's leadership and resourcefulness guided Aloha Airlines through precarious times. One of the most notable was the struggle to maintain local ownership of the airline, culminating in its leveraged buyout in 1987. In this crucial step, Dr. Ching relied heavily on the support of long-time Aloha co-owner and director, Sheridan C.F. Ing. In recognition of his role, Mr. Ing became Aloha's chairman, a post he held until his passing in 1993.

The final chapter in the epic story of Aloha Airlines' pioneers came to a close on March 26, 1996, when, at the age of 83, Hung Wo Ching passed away after a long and valiant struggle with cancer. The end came just four months before Aloha's 50th anniversary. Dr. Ching is sorely missed by all those who knew him and benefited from his sagacity, dedication and rare vision. This book is dedicated to his memory.

Foreword

*N*othing is more fundamental to the American spirit than free enterprise. It is what made the United States the greatest economic power in the world, and is what gives us the strength to lead all others into the next century.

The story of Aloha Airlines is a classic tale of American enterprise—the story of a successful business. At its heart, it is primarily about people who, through their skill, determination and sacrifice, made the business what it is today. Aloha bears the clear imprint of those who dared to build it and nurture it through a melding of toughness, dreams, spirit and style.

Aloha's experience over the past 50 years also makes social and political history. It began as the airline of the people—all people. There was a sense of ownership and inclusion, a sense of aloha. I am proud to have been a part of Aloha's history. Born and raised in Hawaii and a returned veteran of World War II, I witnessed firsthand many of the hardships and sentiments described in the first chapter of this book. While a student at the University of Hawaii, I volunteered as a non-paid sales representative for Aloha—Trans-Pacific Airlines, as it was called then—and was in on its first faltering steps.

Aloha has made great strides since its early and humble beginnings. It witnessed, participated, and in some instances led Hawaii forward into the world class tourist destination and sophisticated business setting of today.

I hope you enjoy reading Aloha's story. It is both remarkable and powerful. I would like to believe that the pioneering philosophy of inclusions and aloha will continue to guide Aloha Airlines forward into the 21st century.

U.S. Senator Daniel K. Inouye

Table of Contents

Chapter 1: Maiden Flight 7

Chapter 2: The People's Airline 15

Chapter 3: Seat of the Pants 21

Chapter 4: The Jet Age 33

Chapter 5: Flying High 43

Chapter 6: Back to Basics 49

Chapter 7: Keeping the Faith 61

Chapter 8: "The Best We Can Possibly Be" 67

Chapter 9: Hawaii's Airline 73

Chapter 10: Positioned for the Long Haul 77

Acknowledgements 85

Index 87

Chapter 1: Maiden Flight

*I*t was an Aloha Friday, back in the days when that meant something special in the Islands. As the morning sun warmed the air hanging limply over nearby Keehi Lagoon, the freshly painted DC-3 taxied to the end of runway 4-Right at John Rodgers Field.

Despite being the end of the work week in Honolulu, it was a quiet day at the city's airport, a complex of concrete runways and cavernous Quonset huts built by the Navy during World War II. The buildings, squatting along Lagoon Drive, were still painted battleship gray. The war in the Pacific had been over less than a year and the many military installations in Hawaii remained, despite the departure of most of the troops.

Some of the discharged Pacific war veterans stayed on. On this Friday morning, two of them, ex-Navy pilots Al Olson and Louis Lucas, sat in the cockpit of the DC-3 idling at the end of the Rodgers Field runway.

At a signal from the control tower, the plane turned into the wind and gunned its twin Pratt & Whitney engines. The throaty roar scattered the snowy white terns and boobies foraging by the runway and echoed across Keehi Lagoon toward Diamond Head, which that morning loomed large and clear on the horizon. Nearer by, Aloha Tower plainly marked the site of Honolulu Harbor. It was still the tallest building in the Islands.

Capt. Al Olson waves from the cockpit of one of TPA's first DC-3s.

the tallest building in the Islands.

The date was July 26, 1946. The occasion was the first revenue-paying flight of a brand-new airline called, with a flourish of confidence typical of the times, Trans-Pacific Airlines.

It wasn't the very first flight for the new airline. Days earlier, its war-sur-

Louise Gonsales and an unidentified friend pose before TPA's first Honolulu terminal.

plus C-47—the military name for the DC-3—had taken a hunting party to Molokai. But those were friends of Trans-Pacific's founder, Honolulu publisher Ruddy Tongg, and they only chipped in for the gas. On July 26, the DC-3, newly painted with TPA's blue and red colors, carried the first full-fledged paying passengers.

The flight was from Honolulu to Hilo and return, a distance of about 200 miles each way. There was an intermediate stop on Maui. The round trip took a good part of the day—an hour and a half of flying time to Hilo and the same coming back, plus the stopovers. Hilo's airport was Lyman Field, also a former military airfield, and Maui's was on another wartime Navy field near the plantation town of Puunene. The passenger, cargo and maintenance facilities at all the fields were in the Navy's corrugated steel Quonset huts. Conditions were Spartan. The passengers sat with the cargo—on and off the plane.

Louis "Captain Luke" Lucas remembers that first flight as if it were yesterday. He flew co-pilot to Al Olson. "The weather was great," he recalls. "I had a little trouble getting the landing gear up after the first takeoff, but otherwise no problems."

Enroute from Honolulu to Maui the plane flew "at about 2,000 feet" along the steep cliffs lining Molokai's north shore, says Lucas. Today, the former pilot, who retired from flying in 1977, lives on Molokai. "It was a great day for sightseeing, and we were in no hurry." The plane circled over waterfalls and swooped over wave-splashed, empty beaches. The passengers loved it.

From Maui to Hilo, the plane gave its passengers a good look at the Hamakua Coast, a solid belt of green sugar cane fields stretching from Waipio Valley to Hilo. "We had a lot of fun," says Lucas. "We had a full load coming back from Hilo, too."

A full load meant, at the time, 21 passengers. The DC-3's seating hadn't yet been changed from the military configuration: metal bucket seats that ran bench like along each side of the fuselage, facing inward. Later, the seats were re-mounted in rows facing forward, which boosted the passenger capacity to 28.

Baggage and cargo were carried in forward bays and behind nets in the rear of the plane, or sometimes lashed up the aisle between the passengers.

The DC-3 was designed before the widespread use of the tricycle landing gear. Its tail rested on the ground like those of all early vintage planes. Boarding near the rear, passengers had to climb to their seats.

The cabin was unpressurized, which kept flights to moderate altitudes. It was good for sightseeing, but the squalls and storms that frequent the Hawaiian Islands had to be flown through, rather than over. The DC-3 was built to handle bad weather, but it could be rough on passengers. "There was a saying about the DC-3, that when it rained outside it poured inside," chuckles "Captain Luke" Lucas, who piloted through rain storms with a newspaper spread over his lap.

And the plane was noisy. Its big radial engines were designed for performance rather than comfort. The roar of a DC-3 under full throttle was unmistakable even at a great distance. To the people inside, it was deafening. Normal conversation was out of the question.

But for the incredible 15 years that it used the DC-3s, Trans-Pacific Airlines and its successor, Aloha Airlines, learned to maximize the legendary airplane's virtues and minimize its faults. "In the '40s and '50s the DC-3 was as much a household name as Ford or Chevy," says Raymond "Spike" Cordero, a TPA mechanic in those days. "Everybody trusted them."

He remembers the early flights. "The first flight out every morning was loaded with Love's bread bound for Molokai and Maui," says Cordero, who retired in 1970. TPA used one of the old Navy Quonset huts along Lagoon Drive for a hangar. The facilities, like the planes, were basic.

But the DC-3 used on TPA's inaugural flight—plane No. 65393—was unusually well-appointed. It had been equipped by the Navy to fly VIPs. Its metal bucket seats were upholstered. "I'm not sure the passengers on that first flight appreciated that," says co-pilot Lucas.

An early TPA sales brochure features two heirlooms: A DC-3 and the 1940s Honolulu waterfront.

The Douglas DC-3, or C-47, had been the workhorse of American and allied armed forces in every theater of World War II. The rugged planes flew the

"Hump" in Burma, dropped paratroops into New Guinea, landed on barely cleared strips in South Pacific jungles. They flew through sandstorms in North Africa, through blizzards in the Ardennes, through flak at Normandy. Wherever the Army and Navy went, the DC-3s were there delivering troops and supplies. Thousands of the planes saw duty. And when the war was over, nearly all of them became surplus.

"There's no question that the ready availability and good prices of these planes was a factor in TPA's start," says David A. Benz, another young veteran who had been hired by Ruddy Tongg as a business manager for his publishing company. The cost of the first three DC-3s bought from Navy surplus by Tongg and his associates was between $20,000 and $25,000 each, including spare parts.

But there were other, deeper reasons for starting the airline.

The Hawaii of 1946 was much the same socially, politically and economically as it had been for more than half a century. After overthrowing the native Hawaiian monarchy in 1893 and getting Hawaii annexed as a U.S. territory, American businessmen, some descended from the New England missionaries who came to the islands 70 years earlier, ran the remote former kingdom like a private fiefdom.

Service aboard a TPA Vistaliner came with flowers and smiles.

Power focused on the "Big Five" companies, which controlled the Islands' sugar industry, the backbone of the economy.

Though the families of the *haole*—Caucasian—elite embraced Western values and culture, the West during the late 19th and early 20th centuries was itself far from a paragon of social and racial equality. And race played an important, though usually unspoken, part in island life. Near the bottom of the social, economic and political ladder were the Oriental residents, whose parents or grandparents had come to Hawaii, first from China and then Japan, as contract laborers on the sugar plantations that then covered the landscape. As time passed, the Orientals moved off the plantations and into the towns, to be replaced by Filipino and other immigrant labor. But the transition was slow and moving off the plantation didn't mean moving up the socio-economic ladder.

While pre-war Hawaii showed the world a picture-postcard view of bronzed, laughing faces, sunlit beaches, swaying palms and soft tropical nights, it was in fact a land of considerable social injustice.

In 1946, Ruddy Tongg and his friends had known discrimination all of their lives. The best schools, the best jobs, the best opportunities, all the things that money and position could buy still went to the *haole* establishment. There were beginning to be exceptions, but not many.

It took World War II to turn the system on its ear. By the end of the

Ruddy Tongg poses with some Australian representatives.

war, there were big changes in the wind. The millions of servicemen who passed through Hawaii during the war and the thousands of island boys who returned from foreign battlefields introduced a new, untraditional view toward life. When Tongg and his associates started Trans-Pacific Airlines it was to test the wings not just of a promising business venture, but also of an independence whose time they sensed had finally come.

Still, TPA was no symbolic gesture. Its founders were tough, pragmatic *Pake*—the Hawaiian word for Chinese—businessmen. They thought the airline's prospects were excellent, especially with all the "locals" solidly behind it. Still, it wasn't long before Tongg asked Dave Benz to "help him out" with TPA. He was discovering there was more to running an airline than having guts, a vision and a few war-surplus airplanes.

TPA didn't have a license to operate scheduled flights. It could only fly charters, which made building revenues a lot harder, especially for a new airline. And nobody who started the company knew anything about operating an airline. Even the pilots' experience was entirely military. Lucas and Olson had flown multi-engine Navy planes. So had George Cullen, another of the early pilots. But that was no deterrent. "There was a feeling after the war that we could do anything," says Cullen.

Another thing TPA didn't have a lot of was money. With passenger revenues coming in slowly and unpredictably, cash was always in short supply. Ruddy Tongg often covered cash shortfalls out of his own pocket. For years, employees would sometimes be asked not to cash their paychecks until there was enough money in the bank to cover them.

"We would always get paid," says Malmorina Snyder—"Mellie" to most everybody who knows her. "Sometimes it just took awhile. But we didn't really mind. We were family. The company was one big *'ohana.*"

Mellie Snyder—her last name was Ricopuerto then—was one of TPA's first flight attendants. Her pay was $100 a month. A workweek sometimes lasted 100 hours. "We didn't have the union then," she smiles. "But we didn't mind the hours or the pay. A lot of us grew up on plantations. We were used to working long and hard. And we were happy to have an exciting job. Most girls with my background had to work as clerks in a store or office." Snyder retired in 1988 and now conducts tours as a volunteer at Honolulu's Iolani Palace.

Nor did early employees mind doing more than their assigned jobs. Helen Imai was hired in 1950 as a reservations clerk in TPA's downtown Honolulu office, then located in the Mitsukoshi Building at King and Bethel Streets. Sometimes she was asked to fill in as a flight attendant. "We didn't mind," she says. "It made our work more interesting."

It also made the workdays longer. For that there wasn't more pay, but occasionally there were other compensations. Ruddy Tongg owned an interest in the Waikiki Tavern, a popular eatery and watering hole. "Now and then Ruddy would give us a free dinner when we worked late," remembers Imai.

Though he was the top boss, Tongg was called by his first name. "Everybody

TPA's King and Bethel Streets office in downtown Honolulu.

went by their first name," says Imai. "We were all family. That's the way we lived then. What we grew up with."

An exception was "Mr. Benz," whose early invitation to "help out" at TPA soon became a full-time commitment. Though trained in publishing, he soon ran the airline operations for Tongg, "who was mostly concerned with sales and other forms of raising money," Benz recalls.

It was a tough job. There were constant money problems. Benz not only had to keep the airline flying but deal with some-

Dave Benz: His short tour at TPA got extended.

times unpaid employees and creditors. Nearly a half-century later, people still speak with awe about the way he juggled the problems.

"Ruddy Tongg had the vision, but Dave Benz made it happen," says Robert "Bob" MacGregor, a veteran Hawaii tourism executive whose tour company was a key early customer of TPA. "Mr. Benz was a good boss," remembers Helen Imai. "He looked tough on the outside, but inside he was a softy. He was very fair to everybody."

That wasn't the case in many Hawaii companies, even after the war. But the changes were coming, led by returning veterans like the much-decorated Japanese-Americans of the 442nd Regimental Combat Team. Still, it wouldn't be until vet-led Democrats won control of the Territorial Legislature in 1954, Hawaii became the 50th state of the Union in 1959, and tourism unseated sugar as the Islands' top industry, breaking the old economic power structure, that the major social changes would come.

Passengers boarding an early TPA flight.

Chapter 2: The People's Airline

*D*ave Benz describes the reasons for TPA's beginnings as socio-economic: "Island people weren't treated too well in those days. They couldn't get choice jobs in the airline industry or anyplace else. Some of Ruddy's friends said they even had trouble getting airline seats. They figured, 'why not start our own airline?'"

But they couldn't even do that the way some others could. "They couldn't borrow the money from the banks," says Benz. "The banks then still wouldn't loan money to Orientals."

Frustrated on many business fronts, local entrepreneurs invented what has since become a Hawaii institution, the investment *hui*—groups of individuals pooling their personal resources.

One man who remembered those days clearly was Dr. Hung Wo Ching, an agricultural economist who built a real estate fortune in Hawaii with the help of *huis*. Dr. Ching was one of the original investors in TPA and in the following decades would become the person most responsible for the airline's success. Interviewed late in 1995, still clear and sharp-wit-

Dr. Hung Wo Ching (l.) looks out of costume at ceremonies ushering out the DC-3.

The Story of Aloha Airlines

15

ted despite his 83 years, Ching recalled that, in the beginning, banks wouldn't lend him money, either.

But by 1946 Hawaii was developing an independent spirit, shaking off its century-old plantation mentality. For the first time, labor unions were organizing workers in the fields, on the docks and even in some offices. The *haole*-dominated territorial oligarchy was losing its grip politically and economically.

Some people at the time said TPA stood for "The People's Airline."

"If you were an Oriental, most companies wouldn't even consider you for the kind of jobs TPA hired us to do," says Elsie Umaki, who worked in reservations in the early years. "We all worked hard. But we all had fun. We had a sense of proprietorship. It was our airline," she says.

Handling reservations was a slow process then. The clerks sat around a large, round table and posted reservations on cards that were placed in a circular file that rotated in the center of the table, like a "lazy Susan." The table resembled, and in fact might once have been, the type found in Chinese restaurants. "Everything was done by phone and by hand," says Umaki. "We would even make hotel and rent-a-car reservations for passengers—free, just as an extra service." Elsie's husband, Roy Umaki, was the first Oriental pilot hired by TPA or, possibly, any other domestic U.S. airline.

Some other Japanese-Americans got their start with TPA and went on to other fields. One was Daniel K. Inouye, a wounded veteran of the 442nd who returned after the war to finish his undergraduate education at the University

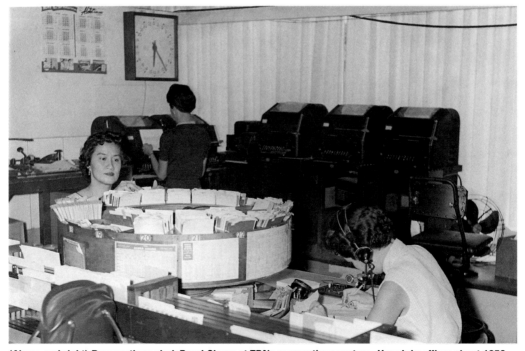

(Above and right) Reservations clerk Pearl Chong at TPA's reservations system, Honolulu office; about 1950.

of Hawaii. He asked his family friend Ruddy Tongg for a job. Tongg said he didn't have any. Inouye, anxious for the experience, said he would work for nothing. He had the GI Bill and a disability pension from the Army and didn't really need the extra money.

Tongg "hired" young Inouye and put him to work part time selling tickets on the UH campus, among veterans groups and to the small storekeepers that then dotted the Honolulu landscape. "It was great experience; I learned how to meet and talk to people," says Inouye, who later left to go to law school, returned to help lead the 1954 Democratic revolt in the Territorial Legislature, and who has represented Hawaii in the U.S. Senate since 1963.

Pat Fukuda was also an undergraduate at the UH when she and three other co-eds got what was for them an offer of a lifetime. Ruddy Tongg asked if they would fill in on weekends as flight attendants. By bringing in part-time help, TPA could give its full-time attendants some time off without having to hire more of them.

But, like salesman Inouye, this, too, was a win-win situation. "We were delighted," recalls Pat, the former part-timer. "We had a blast. My friends were jealous. Here I was flying all over the Islands every weekend, and getting paid for it." She doesn't remember how much she was paid, "but I know it helped."

Fukuda became a teacher, got married, changed her last name to Saiki, and went into local politics. In 1986 she was elected as one of Hawaii's two members of the U.S. House of Representatives, becoming only the second

Republican the state's voters have ever sent to Washington.

"Our employees were special. They knew they were special. They were making history here. They were Hawaii's golden people in a golden era." The words aren't carved on a monument somewhere, but flow freely from a person some people say was as important to the start of TPA as Ruddy Tongg or Dave Benz. He is Richard "Dick" King, who for almost 25 years was the man most responsible for selling "the people's airline" to the traveling public.

King talks about his life as a series of "educations." An urbane, easy talking product of Washington society—his father once headed the U.S. Secret Service—King's education began at Dartmouth in the 1930s. During the war, he flew multi-engine planes for the Navy and finished on the staff of the colorful Adm. William F. "Bull" Halsey. He mustered out of the Navy in Hawaii and, using war surplus DC-3s, helped start a fledgling air cargo company called Trans Air Hawaii. A specialty was flying fresh vegetables to Honolulu from Maui and Molokai and fresh fish from French Frigate Shoals.

When Trans Air ran into financial squalls, King accepted a job with TPA. But his talents lay outside the cockpit. "After a while, I sort of ran everything aft of the cockpit operationally, and I took over marketing because there was nobody else to do it," says King, relaxing on the lanai of the Hilo home he retired to in the 1980s, after completing yet another learning experience with American Express Co. He left the airline in 1971 with a long string of accomplishments. But what people remember most about Dick King was his flair for promotion, especially in the early days.

"Dick not only put the airline on the map, he put Hawaii on the map," says Robert C. Allen, who headed the Hawaii Visitors Bureau when it was still counting annual tourist arrivals in six digits.

Trans-Pacific Airlines got its name because Ruddy Tongg and his associates had early ambitions of air routes to China. Hung Wo Ching went to China after the war to try to start a sugar industry there. But the Communist revolution soon put a stop to all their plans. Dr. Ching came home to develop real estate in Honolulu and TPA concentrated on flying between the Hawaiian Islands. It was a concentration that served it well in later years.

In smaller print beneath the TPA logo in the '40s was the legend, "The Aloha Airline." It was an afterthought for Tongg and his investors, but Dick King saw it as a marketing opportunity.

So did Bob MacGregor, who first arrived in Hawaii on a China Clipper in 1936. He worked for the Clipper's owner, Pan American World Airways, through the war years and in 1950 settled in Honolulu and started Trade Wind Tours, catering to the still embryonic U.S. travel market. His office was on King and

Souvenir flight packet of the early '50s, showing TPA's inter-island routes.

Bethel Streets, across the intersection from TPA's office in the Mitsukoshi Building.

"I was convinced that Hawaii had a great future in tourism," says MacGregor, who, though now in his 80s, still pursues a lifelong passion for polo.

In 1951 MacGregor attended a meeting at the Moana Hotel. At the time, the Moana was a half-century old, which made it the oldest of the handful of hotels then located on Waikiki Beach. It and the next-door Royal Hawaiian Hotel belonged to Matson Navigation Co., which still brought most of Hawaii's visitors from the Mainland on its steamships.

At the meeting besides MacGregor were representatives of Matson, Pan Am, Trans World Airways and the Hawaii Visitors Bureau. Pan Am and TWA were America's only international airlines. Hawaii, a mind-numbing 12 hours' flying time from the West Coast, was considered an international destination. MacGregor recalls the Moana meeting very clearly. The subject was, "What does Hawaii have to do to attract 100,000 visitors a year."

It was a tall order. In 1951, the annual visitor count was less than 50,000.

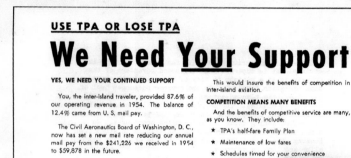

This appeal appeared on the back of a letter to TPA's local stockholders in 1955.

Chapter 3: Seat of the Pants

*A*ttracting more visitors to Hawaii wasn't TPA's greatest concern at the time. Practically from the beginning it became apparent that, in order to survive, the airline needed more than a license to fly charters. It applied to the U.S. Civil Aeronautics Board, then the airline industry's top regulator, for a Certificate of Convenience and Necessity, which would have enabled the company to provide scheduled service.

But, even with the post-war airline industry expanding rapidly, TPA faced some large obstacles. For one thing, Hawaii being a U.S. territory, starting scheduled operations there required the approval of the U.S. President. In the late '40s, Island politics were still heavily Republican, a legacy of the Big Five, and the U.S. President was Harry S. Truman, a staunch Democrat. TPA didn't have the money to pay for a major lobbying effort in Washington.

The biggest hurdle, however, was TPA's competition. All the commercial passenger flying between the Hawaiian Islands in 1946 was done by a company called Inter-Island Airlines, a subsidiary of Inter-Island Steam Navigation Co. The parent company was a product of the old plantation days and had dominated surface travel between the islands for decades. When the airline subsidiary was launched in 1929 with a fleet of bi-winged Sikorsky seaplanes, it also had the inter-island routes all to itself.

Hung Wo Ching remembered flying in one of the Sikorskys to Kauai when he was a boy and having to sit in a stairwell, where he was drenched during the waterborne takeoffs and landings. According to Ching and others, that sort of treatment wasn't unusual for the times. Inter-Island Airlines discriminated against Orientals in

Ruddy Tongg speaking at ceremonies marking TPA's first scheduled flight, 1949.

A bird's-eye view of the scheduled flight ceremonies, Honolulu's Rodgers Field. Note the uninterrupted view of the Waianae Range.

its hiring and other practices. "They had a few Hawaiians working for them, but the rest were Caucasians," recalls Dave Benz. Still, while challenging old prejudices may have been one reason for starting TPA, says Benz, undoubtedly the biggest reason was the economic growth that everybody saw on Hawaii's post-war horizon.

In some ways, TPA had an even playing field in competing with Inter-Island Airlines. From 1946 until the mid-'50s, both flew the same equipment, DC-3s. Of course, Inter-Island had the advantages of being an established carrier, and TPA was an upstart. But easily Inter-Island's biggest edge was its scheduled service. It became apparent nearly from the start that, to survive, TPA had to obtain the same status.

"Getting certification was my top priority when Ruddy Tongg brought me over to the airline," says Benz. "I started a succession of commutes to Washington that was to last several years."

Inter-Island Airlines fought TPA's certification bid tooth and nail. The fight spilled over into the courts. Inter-Island got an injunction that virtually shut TPA down for more than a year by claiming it was using its charter license to fly scheduled service. TPA countered with an anti-trust lawsuit accusing Inter-Island of monopolistic practices.

Inter-Island finally had its injunction overturned, but not until it had cost TPA dearly in lost revenues. TPA won its anti-trust suit, but failed in a lengthy effort to collect damages. The net result of the court battles was undoubtedly more harmful to TPA, since it could afford the legal skirmishing far less than its rival.

By 1949 TPA was strapped financially. The company had no credit, revenues were down because of a six-month-long dock strike, and debts mounted. But early in the year good news came from Washington. On February 17, 1949, President Truman signed a temporary certificate permitting TPA to start scheduled flights. Dave Benz says congressional Democrats, headed by House leader Sam Rayburn, prevailed on the President. The Republicans had won control of Congress and the Democrats were looking for support wherever they could get it, even in a voteless territory.

But the badly wanted certificate by no means took TPA out of the woods. The 1949 dock strike throttled the Hawaii economy, slowing all inter-island commerce. And flying scheduled service meant reorganizing the airline, re-training flight and ground personnel, developing new procedures and acquiring new equipment. TPA had little money to do these things, but in four months of round-the-clock efforts it managed them. Ruddy Tongg once again called on investors and came up with enough money to carry the company through the transition. "Everybody pitched in," remembers Mellie Snyder. "We

A "typical" Vistaliner cabin crew.

got more rubber paychecks, but that didn't seem to matter."

TPA had also applied to carry U.S. mail. Approval would bring it a mail subsidy that was designed to help struggling airlines. But the mail application, like the certification request, was kept pending for some time. Rival Inter-Island Airlines fought that as hard as it had TPA's scheduled service. "They didn't want us around, period," says Dick King.

Meantime, TPA's rival had changed its name. Its parent Inter-Island Steam Navigation Co. split up and the airline carried on as Hawaiian Airlines. And, with flights from the Mainland now arriving regularly, local authorities abandoned the old Lagoon Drive Quonset huts and moved facilities across the runway to establish Honolulu International Airport.

The approval of TPA's request to carry the mail finally came through, but not until 1951. By then, TPA, calling itself TPA Aloha Airlines, was benefiting from a recovering Hawaii economy and the sort of tourism hopes reflected in the meeting Bob MacGregor attended that year at the Moana Hotel.

But amid the optimism were problems. The Korean War was causing shortages in aircraft parts and boosting fuel costs. In the first nine months of 1951, TPA's operating expenses jumped from $1.04 per revenue mile to $1.24, then fell to 92 cents when the company made new cutbacks. Nevertheless, that year TPA Aloha had the lowest net loss in its short history—$40,000, versus an accumulated $364,000 deficit only two years before.

Things were looking up, and Dick King unleashed a barrage of new promotions to boost business. TPA's flight attendants not only plied passengers with pineapple juice—an innovation from the company's charter days—but entertainment. "I think we had to sing, dance the hula and play the ukulele to get a job," says Mellie Snyder, trying to remember the details. "That's right," confirms King, who probably made the rules.

Another carryover from the charter operations were the special volcano flights. When the Big Island's Kilauea Volcano erupted—an unusual event in those days—the company would add flights to tour the eruption. Panoramic windows—five feet wide—gave passengers better views and gave Dick King a new name to promote: "Vistaliners." "Camera *pukas*"—openings in the windows through which camera lenses could be thrust—were another innovation.

"Two of the DC-3's major features were that it flew low and slow," explains King. "The wide windows, the *pukas*, the singing stewardesses—these and other things were done to take advantage of those features," he says, still with the sure smile of a born promoter.

Attendant Mellie Snyder, center, with some enthusiastic in-flight entertainers.

Sometimes even the pilots got into the spirit of the tours. Peter Economou, another former Navy flier who became TPA's chief pilot in the 1950s and later a senior executive, flew so close to one eruption the heat cracked a window in the DC-3's cockpit, recalls "Captain Luke" Lucas.

Using the Vistaliner's handy *puka*.

"Those volcano flights were pretty exciting," says Pat Saiki. "We had to learn the names of all the waterfalls we'd see along the way because we'd take those in, too."

King didn't confine the entertainment to TPA's flights. He took troupes of entertainers—all company employees—to Mainland travel shows and conventions. When there weren't shows he would stage his own. Before long, TPA Aloha Airlines became known to travel agents and tour organizers nationwide.

Its fame spread to other entertainers. Frank Sinatra called for the Aloha troupe when he came to Hawaii to film "From Here to Eternity." Other celebrities asked for them, too. And as the group became known, so did the airline. John Wayne flew TPA on and off the screen when he visited to make the 1952 movie "Big Jim McLain." Leonard Bernstein, then conductor of the New York Philharmonic Orchestra, invited the Aloha group to entertain his whole ensemble during a world tour stopover in Honolulu. Then the orchestra entertained the troupe with its

TPA entertainers Ululani Kealoha (l.) and Dona Kualii. They sold not only the airline, but the Islands.

In the late '50s the newly renamed Aloha Airlines was a hit with the stars. Clockwise from top-left, Frank Sinatra, John Wayne, Jane Russell and Esther Williams, Howard Duff and Ida Lupino, Shirley Temple Black (with husband Charles Black), Sen. John F. Kennedy, Lana Turner and friends, and "Hawaiian Eye's" Poncy Ponce.

Original Kona Airport, with its vintage Quonset hut terminal; 1950s.

version of Hawaiian music. The orchestra next hired four TPA planes to fly all its members to Maui and back. Dick King calls this sort of thing "planting seeds."

Robert Allen, who headed the Hawaii Visitors Bureau in the '60s, says Art Lewis, then president of Hawaiian Airlines, asked him one day what Hawaiian should do to increase revenues. "I told him he should hire Dick King," says Allen. He didn't and perhaps regretted it.

Other company employees picked up on King's flair for innovation. Clifford Bowman, the company's station manager in rainy Hilo, developed a portable shed to shelter passengers walking between the terminal and planes. Bowman and personnel at other stations would sometimes dress as Native Hawaiians to welcome passengers.

One of the most successful promotions was the "family fare." If a family member bought a ticket at the full price, everybody else in the family could fly for half-fare. "Hawaiian Airlines fought that one, too," smiles King. "But it stuck. It was very popular. It did a lot for our revenues. That might have been the first inter-island fare discount program." If it was, many more were to follow.

In 1952, TPA Aloha Airlines made its first profit: $36,410.12. The company still reported its financial results to the cent. That year, TPA carried 175,000 passengers—a 26 percent gain from the year before. The company operated five DC-3 "Alohaliners," as King was calling them at the time. Its share of the inter-is-

New planes brought new routes. This map is from the early '60s.

land airline market was about 30 percent—up from 10 percent just two years before. "Dave Benz used to say things would be okay if we had 30 percent of the market," recalls Elsie Umaki.

But things weren't yet okay. Though it continued to show profits, the company still struggled. Expenses continued to climb, despite ongoing efforts to contain them and to increase revenues. The company was cited by the National Safety Council for its accident-free record—another mark of the emphasis on quality service and the start of a long tradition. But safety, too, carries a price and TPA's operating costs were catching up with revenues.

The biggest challenge came from technology. Newer planes were outperforming the venerable DC-3. Hawaiian Airlines ordered new twin-engine Convairs that had tricycle landing gears and pressurized cabins. The planes would give Hawaiian advantages that TPA, with its plodding, leaky, noisy DC-3s, couldn't hope to match. And, though still in another part of the world, commercial jet travel had become a reality. Before long, that, too, would reach Hawaii. Seat of the pants flying was fast going out of style.

Ted Kagoshima, now an executive with TPA's successor Aloha Airlines, says the industry has lost something since the days he joined it in the late '50s. "Everybody knew everybody else in the industry then," he says. "There was a warm relationship between the airlines, the hotels and the agents."

Sakai "Andy" Yamashiro joined TPA as a mechanic in 1949 and stayed for 38 years. Now he tends the roses outside his sunny Kahala home. For years, his pay from the airline wasn't enough to support his family so he moonlighted, hiring out in his spare time as a mechanic to the many airlines that transited Honolulu in the old propeller era. "All together I was bringing home around $150 a month—which was considered good money in those days," says Yamashiro.

"It was hard work, but the work was steady," says the retired mechanic. "We all felt the airline was finally there to stay." In 1956, Republican President Dwight D. Eisenhower, perhaps with motives similar to Harry Truman's, made TPA's certification permanent.

Mellie Snyder, TPA's senior stewardess, was still earning $100 a month. But she was about to get a raise.

Serving some future stars aboard a Vistaliner: Keola and Kapono Beamer with mom, Winona; about 1955.

Chapter 4: The Jet Age

One day in 1957 Dave Benz paid Hung Wo Ching a personal visit. "He asked me if I would be interested in taking over the airline," recalled Dr. Ching some 38 years later. He was. And by everybody's reckoning, Ching probably saved TPA Aloha Airlines from oblivion.

Early in 1958, the economist-turned-financier became the airline's president and chief executive officer. Ruddy Tongg stayed on as chairman. Dave Benz lingered a few months to teach Ching the airline business, and then returned, probably gratefully, to run Tongg's publishing company—nearly 12 years after being borrowed from that job to "help out" at TPA.

The first thing Ching did was to change the airline's name. Dick King had long wanted to drop the "TPA" name altogether. Ching agreed and the company became simply "Aloha Airlines."

Next came a harder chore, strengthening the company's sagging balance sheet. Ching did that by selling more stock—at first, for 25 cents a share. The results made the company look a little better on paper—enough to impress at least one Honolulu banker. Ching told the story this way:

John Bellinger, an up-and-coming executive at what was to become First Hawaiian Bank, asked new CEO Ching if his airline needed money. Ching, who had learned to do very well without bank loans up to then, said he looked Bellinger in the eye and answered "yes, about $2 million."

"Bellinger asked me if I would personally guarantee such a loan," recalled Ching. "I said yes and he promptly loaned us the money. I didn't dare tell my wife what I had done."

Ching also borrowed $2.3 million from another new institutional source, insurance companies. The financing was crucial to completing the next big change he brought to the airline, new airplanes.

Recognizing that Aloha's aged DC-3s were no match for Hawaiian Air 's new Convairs, Ching ordered a fleet of new Fairchild F-27s. The planes' wings were mounted high, out of the way for sightseeing. They carried 44 passengers—16 more than the DC-3s. Their cabins were pressurized, the same as the Convairs. And they were also propjets, which the Convairs weren't. Aloha got

The Fairchild F-27:
A new plane at Honolulu
International Airport;
1959.

a slight edge on Hawaiian in a competitive race that was just warming up.

The F-27s, introduced in 1959, were an instant success. Aloha's passenger load factor—the best measure of its business—topped 63 percent. Its share of the inter-island air passenger market climbed to 40 percent, a record.

The larger, faster F-27s meant more work for Aloha's flight attendants. So Mellie Snyder and the others got a raise. She then made $125 a month.

The initiation of F-27 service and phase out of the DC-3s started a decade of aircraft changes for Aloha. The transition was propelled by technological advances, by the explosive growth of Hawaii's tourist market, and by fierce competition from Aloha's older, fatter, but now thoroughly aroused competitor, Hawaiian Air.

Hawaiian had teased Aloha in earlier years with some less than sincere overtures to buy out the struggling airline. But now it made what appeared to be an earnest offer. Hung Wo Ching was asked if he would accept a buyout for what could amount to $1.5 million. The actual figure, however, would be determined by an appraisal. Ching figured the appraisal could be much lower than the $1.5 million mentioned and rejected the offer.

Starting them young: Aloha's 1967 poster girl, Cheryl Jung.

"They would have waited until we shut down, then done their appraisal on a failed airline," said Ching. "I wasn't going to bite." But he would have an opportunity in the future to reconsider.

In 1959, after years of trying, Hawaii was admitted as the 50th state in the Union. Statehood had an immediate stimulating effect on the Islands' econ-

omy. New investments flowed in from Mainland financial institutions as entrepreneurs
flocked to the Aloha State bent on mining for-
tunes from its golden beaches.

But probably the biggest economic stimu-
lant had little to do with statehood. The same year,
some major U.S. airlines began jet service between
the West Coast and Honolulu, cutting the flying
time in half. That event more than any other
made Hawaii's visitor industry what it is today.

Aloha Airlines got its new airplanes just in
time to get in on the ground floor of the tourism surge. But soon it had another equipment
problem. While the F-27s were popular, flexible
and reliable, they weren't large enough to meet the soaring need
for seats.

An Aloha Airlines aloha shirt.

The trouble was, other airlines faced the same problem and the demand for
passenger jets exceeded the supply. The push was on for all-jet planes built for
the short-haul market, such as the inter-island service. But tiny Aloha couldn't
compete in the aircraft marketplace with giants like United Airlines, American and
TWA. So it looked for an answer in the secondary aircraft market, where it had
obtained the F-27.

**Two generations of Aloha aircraft in the early '60s: Foreground, the F-27, and behind it, two Vickers
Viscounts.**

A Vickers Viscount getting a checkup in Aloha's maintenance hanger, Honolulu International Airport, mid-1960s.

In 1963 the company introduced to its inter-island routes the British-built Vickers Viscount, a four-engine propjet that carried 56 passengers. But the shiny, sleek-looking planes were an immediate flop with both passengers and crews.

"It flew like a truck," says "Captain Luke" Lucas. Despite its four engines, the Viscount was "the most grossly under-powered plane I ever flew. It kept wandering and you'd have to re-point it." Passengers didn't like it because the cabin was cramped.

When another British plane, the all-jet BAC-111, became available in the mid-'60s Aloha jumped at the chance to try them. The 111 had twin-jet engines mounted in the tail and carried 80 passengers. It seemed ideal for the inter-island market. But Hawaiian Airlines ordered the Douglas DC-9, a brand-new answer to the short-haul demand that seated more than 100 passengers, giving Hawaiian a big advantage in inter-island capacity.

When it also turned out that the BAC-111's lifting capability wouldn't permit it to take off from the short runway in Kona with a full load, Aloha looked elsewhere for an answer to the DC-9.

It came from McDonnell Douglas' chief rival in the airliner business, The Boeing Co. Boeing had pioneered commercial jet travel with the 707, a commercialized version of the bombers and tankers it built for the U.S. Air Force. And it got a lock on the global intermediate-range passenger jet market with the tri-jet 727. Then in the late 1960s it introduced its entry to the short-range market, the twin-jet 737. Some say the 737 is equaled only by the legendary DC-3 for the impact it has had on the airline industry.

Aloha's attraction to the Boeing 737 was a case of love at first flight. The planes carried 118 passengers with ease, comfort and jet-age speed. When Aloha acquired all it could and introduced the first 737s to its inter-island routes in 1969 they were an immediate hit with passengers, cabin crews and, importantly, pilots. "The 737 is the best plane I ever flew, bar none," says Captain Luke Lucas, whose history with airplanes goes back to the open-air Grumman biplanes he flew in the pre-war Navy.

Just before it launched 737 service, Aloha's advertising proclaimed "The Wonderful New World of Aloha Airlines." The company was introducing not only a new airplane, but a whole new image.

John McDermott remembers the occasion. At the time he headed one of Hawaii's largest advertising agencies, Fawcett & McDermott. The agency had been trying to get regular business out of Aloha for years, but until then the company had done most of its own advertising work. Suddenly there was an opening.

Songmaster Jack DeMello (l.) going over his "Wonderful World of Aloha" theme song with the airline's marketing chief, Dick King.

"They wanted to make a big splash with their new planes," remembers McDermott, now silver-haired, tanned, long retired from the ad business and a writer of travel books. "We developed a whole package for them and presented it to their board in the ballroom of the Royal Hawaiian Hotel."

He reconstructs the scene. "Our program had everything: new designs for their planes inside and out; new uniforms for their people; new ads; new commercials; new slogans; new songs by Jack Demello; the works. The president of Boeing paled at our new designs for the planes, but Aloha's board loved every bit of it. The only exception was the white pants we'd designed for the men. Hung Wo Ching thought they would be impractical."

Advertising the Funbirds, 1970.

The new 737s were called "Funbirds." Their 22-foot tails were painted with a spray of bright orange, gold and yellow plumeria. "Flower Power"—a catchy expression of the period—was a campaign theme. But there was a delay in delivery of the new Boeing planes and Aloha lost revenues and market share to Hawaiian's new DC-9s. The result was an operating loss for 1968.

Aloha pressed several of the new 737s into service in 1969 and began phasing out its BAC-111s and

Rolling out a Boeing 737 Funbird in the early '70s: An instant hit all around.

Viscounts. It looked like the new planes had arrived in the nick of time. A series of Pacific route awards late in 1968 had more than doubled the number of U.S. carriers authorized to serve Hawaii. The awards came just as the big airlines were upping their capacities with new wide-bodied Boeing 747s and Douglas DC-10s.

But, soon after his inauguration in January 1969, President Richard M. Nixon ordered a re-evaluation of the Pacific route awards. The CAB dutifully reviewed its notes while the new routes were put on ice. In July, it reaf-

"Flower power" planes and uniforms, mid-'70s.

firmed its decision and Western, Continental, Braniff, American and TWA were cleared to join United and Pan Am in serving Hawaii. But by then, most of the newcomers had diverted aircraft to other routes and it wasn't until September that the first of them started Mainland-Hawaii service. That was too late for the summer tourist season and a lot of Islanders were disappointed.

"Hawaii Five-O's" Steve McGarrett (Jack Lord) and friends hop off a Funbird, about 1970.

For some, the disappointment was especially hard, as the visitor boom seemingly signaled by the route awards failed to materialize. With a more than 50 percent increase in capacity brought by the new 737s, plus the planes' cost and the expenses of the marketing campaign, Aloha was particularly hard-hit. Its losses in 1969 more than doubled those of '68.

In 1970, Hawaiian Airlines once again broached the subject of merger. Hawaiian's principal owner and CEO, John Magoon, proposed a merged airline owned 51 percent by Hawaiian's stockholders and 49 percent by Aloha's. But the airline itself would be largely Hawaiian. Aloha was to get rid of its existing 737s and cancel orders for new ones. The merged airline would fly Hawaiian's DC-9s. Most of its personnel would be former Hawaiian employees. Aloha would be shrunk to the point of extinction.

There was an agreement in principal to these terms. Hung Wo Ching and Magoon sought the necessary approvals in Washington. Aloha canceled its new jet orders at Boeing—at a hefty penalty—and started paring back operations.

Then Magoon changed his mind. According to Ching, he told the astonished Aloha executive that his investment advisors wanted to know why he should go to the trouble and expense of merging with Aloha when the rival airline was about to go out of business anyway. The assessment wasn't far off the mark, though Aloha was simply sticking to its end of the merger agreement in winding down operations. In 1971 Magoon walked away from the merger and left Aloha to die.

But it didn't. In fact, Aloha rebounded to a banner year in 1972.

Chapter 5: Flying High

*A*loha faced two major problems with the collapse of the merger. Either was potentially fatal. One was nearly $7 million in debts and the heavy payment schedule that entailed. The other was the reduction of its fleet. To comply with the tentative merger agreement, Aloha had canceled orders for new 737s. That left it with just three of the jets in service, plus some old Viscounts it hadn't yet been able to sell.

But, by leasing 737s from other airlines, juggling its debts, working out a new scheduling agreement for inter-island service and some other stabilizing moves, the losses stemming from the failed merger were halted. "All of a sudden we realized we were on our own, and the only way we could make it was to pull together," says Bert Thomas, who had just replaced the veteran Dick King as Aloha's marketing chief.

"I remember those times," says Baba Kea, a Honolulu fashion designer who had done over the Aloha uniforms. "I wasn't with the company, but I knew their people very well. They were marvelous people. So caring. They worked so closely together, there didn't seem to be anything they couldn't do."

Kenneth F.C. Char, a lawyer-turned-businessman recruited by Hung Wo Ching in the late '50s and later installed as Aloha's president, talked to all the employees about the company's challenge. Keeping in close touch with the employees was a Char trademark, and the rapport and mutual trust it developed paid off in the precarious months after the aborted merger. "He was a sharp guy," says adman John McDermott. "He was a very stabilizing influence."

Aloha Chairman Hung Wo Ching (l.) and President Kenneth Char talking over the merits of the 737.

With the Funbirds, along with everything else came more entertainers.

Aloha reported a net loss in 1971 of $826,000. That was down sharply from a loss of $2.4 million the year before. And most of the '71 deficit came from debt service, indicating a brisk improvement in operating income. As 1972 began, Aloha's outlook brightened noticeably. It sold the last of its Viscounts, giving it a uniform fleet of 737s. In the first quarter of the new year, passenger traffic climbed 52 percent and the airline's load factor shot to 57 percent from as low as 43 percent the previous year.

That year there was a 23 percent rise in Hawaii's visitor count, bringing 2.2 million tourists to the Islands. Aloha benefited handsomely from the gain. But other factors helped, too. So-called "common fare" agreements had been reached among the airlines flying the tourists from the Mainland, making inter-island travel part of the air fare package. Hilo had been opened as a second gateway for the Mainland flights. There was talk of building new airports on the neighbor islands to replace the relics from the DC-3 days. The last American troops were returning from Vietnam, ending one of the most painful eras in the country's history.

With new hotels sprouting in Waikiki and elsewhere, and new office buildings changing the skyline in downtown Honolulu, the construction crane won the title of honorary state bird. Even another economically punishing dock strike didn't halt the prosperity sweeping the Islands. Aloha ended 1972 with a $1.4 million profit—emphatically reversing four straight years of losses. Its share of the inter-island passenger market rose to 41 percent from the low 30s.

"That was a major turnaround," says Bert Thomas. "It may have been the most important year in the company's history. We felt we were on our way at last, and we never looked back."

In 1973 the company reported profits of $3.5 million, thanks to additions to its 737 fleet and another bumper crop of tourists. The profits reflected a 22 percent gain in passenger traffic and a 61.8 percent load factor. But, as always, the good news was mixed with some bad. Late in 1973 the Arab oil embargo sent fuel prices skyrocketing.

Still, riding two good years of tourism, Ken Char and others at Aloha expected 1974 to bring more gains in revenues and profits. This was despite the ominous trend in jet fuel costs, which had climbed 71 percent in the last year—mostly since the oil embargo.

In 1974, Aloha's fuel costs doubled and rose from 8 percent of total operating expenses to 14 percent. The year brought the highest passenger load factor ever—64.2 percent—but the jump in fuel costs had raised the airline's break-even point. What was worse, Hawaii's blistering growth rate in tourists was nearly stalled by the economic recession that grew out of the energy crisis. In 1975, the state's visitor arrivals increased just 1.5 percent—a far cry from the double-digit growth of the 1960s and recent '70s. The local visitor industry, having geared up for a continued surge, was once again caught flat-footed.

Still, by trimming operations wherever it could—by now the company was adept at that—Aloha managed a 65.1 percent passenger load factor in 1975. It was one of the best performances in the whole airline industry. But costs had gone up, too. The company's break-even stood at a load factor of 64.2 percent, leaving very little margin for comfort.

A 1976 ad announces a milestone.

At about this time the company got a new director. He was Stuart T.K. Ho, a prominent Honolulu financier and son of Chinn Ho, whose fame matched that of Hung Wo Ching in Hawaii's galaxy of business greats. "My first impression of Aloha Airlines was how strapped they were," smiles Ho. "Everything was zero-based budgeting, long before the time when that was a popular management tool. But there was nothing elective about it at Aloha."

Nevertheless, management felt confident as Aloha approached its 30th anniversary, which matched almost exactly America's bicentennial. The good news was that the airline had paid off the worst of its debts, it was profitable, its business was growing, it was garnering one national award after another for the reliability and quality of its service, and Aloha had finally won a court victory over its rival Hawaiian Air.

When Hawaiian pulled the rug from under the 1970-71 merger plans, Aloha sued it for anti-trust violations, claiming, with considerable merit, that Hawaiian staged the merger just to maneuver Aloha out of business. Early in 1975 a federal court agreed and awarded Aloha $4.5 million in damages. It took more than a year to collect, however, and then Aloha had to settle on just $1,850,000, paid over three years.

New outfits for the late '70s: Flower Power in 25 striking combinations.

Still, the settlement was a victory and it pleased Chairman Ching's sense of justice. He okayed another company face-lifting: a brighter floral color scheme for the planes and new uniforms for flight and ground personnel. This time, designer Baba Kea gave the employees versatile ensembles. Flight attendants' outfits could be worn in 25 striking combinations.

By 1976 Aloha's impressive performance had attracted the attention of a California company called International Air Service Co.—IASCO, for short. It was flush with cash from a profitable airliner leasing business and was looking for promising investments. IASCO officials notified Aloha's board that they intended to obtain control of the Hawaii company by buying a majority of its stock on the open market.

Share prices zoomed on the news, but IASCO never bought the promised majority. Over time, it did acquire enough stock—about 13 percent of the total

50 Years of Aloha

shares outstanding—to place three directors on Aloha's board. But that didn't amount to control and Aloha eventually bought back all of the IASCO shares.

The IASCO episode was significant more as a harbinger than as a major chapter in Aloha's history. The California company was among the first of a succession of Mainland-based corporate suitors to come courting in Hawaii. It was the beginning of the era of the takeover, an epic period in American business that would alter forever the way big companies operate. That IASCO chose Aloha as its target was probably a high tribute to the airline's potential.

President Edward E. Swofford: Just in time for deregulation.

And the IASCO encounter taught Aloha some valuable lessons that wouldn't be forgotten in the years just ahead.

But there were other challenges nearer at hand. Operating costs were growing again—including this time big increases in labor costs. New contracts with Aloha's now unionized employees had brought sizable raises in pay and benefits. And just around the corner was another fuel crisis.

In September, 1977, Aloha made several management changes, topped by the appointment of a new chief executive. Ken Char was moved to the new post of vice chairman and veteran Pan Am executive Edward E. Swofford was hired to replace him as president and CEO. Swofford arrived just in time for the raft of changes taking shape in the company, as well as a blockbuster that was about to rock the entire airline industry.

For some time, Congress had been under pressure to ease the heavy, often antiquated rules that regulated every aspect of the domestic airline business. Other red tape-bound industries, notably banking, were also being scrutinized. "Deregulation" had become a popular buzz-word in Washington. But of all the changes that resulted, none was greater than those to the airline industry.

Effective in November, 1978, Congress with a stroke of the pen removed most of the regulations that had bound the country's airlines since their inception. So drastic was the change that no one, including the industry experts who had touted deregulation as vital to the country's health, could know what it would bring.

Airlines were suddenly free to grow or shrink as they wished; to fly where they wanted, when they wanted; to charge what fares and offer whatever incentives suited them; to start new airlines whenever they had the means; to shut down old airlines without warning. In short, the airline business changed from a tightly regulated chess match to a free-for-all, a no-holds-barred commercial donneybrook, and it happened almost overnight.

The whole idea behind deregulation was that it would stimulate competition among airlines and thereby benefit their customers with lower fares and better service. After nearly two decades of upheaval, industry observers still argue about whether deregulation has lived up to its billing.

It has clearly affected travel in many ways. It brought new names to the airline industry and erased others, as a wave of consolidations swept the country's carriers. Uninhibited by red tape, new airlines sprouted like weeds. Old ones, household names like Pan Am, Western, National, Eastern, Braniff and Frontier, faded and disappeared.

Among the other obvious results, the volume of air travel has more than doubled since 1978. Much of the increase is due to the attractive cost of flying, which has remained remarkably low despite often soaring costs. In that sense, deregulation has fulfilled its promise. Competition, as new and old carriers battled for passengers with cheap fares, super discounts and generous frequent-flier awards, has kept the lid on air fares—tightly.

But that has produced deregulation's downside: Fewer carriers have meant fewer travel choices, crowded terminals, packed airplanes, tight flight schedules, punitive ticketing policies and other measures taken by the surviving airlines to cut expenses in order to afford their bargain fares.

The big question still being pondered by the experts is whether, in balance, it has all been worth it for consumers.

Chapter 6: Back to Basics

Perhaps the strongest, or at least most tempting, benefit for the airlines in deregulation was how easy it made opening new routes, and even new airlines.

In Hawaii, the new route advantage was largely nullified by geography and the nature of the market. But starting new airlines has proved an irresistible temptation.

In March 1981 a group of former Hawaiian Air executives launched a new inter-island airline. It was called Mid Pacific Airlines. Using a fleet of decade-old turboprops and non-union workers the backers felt they could capture a chunk of the inter-island market with steeply reduced fares and frequent, bare-bones service.

The move came at a time when both the Hawaii economy and the visitor market were feeling the effects of a national recession that was labeled the worst since the Great Depression of the 1930s. Tourism growth had stalled and actually slipped into a decline. Airline operating costs had skyrocketed with another wave of fuel price increases. Aloha actually earned a profit that year, but was one of the few airlines in the country that did. Still, the last thing it needed was a new competitor.

Within weeks of starting, Mid Pacific had captured 8 percent of the inter-island market. So far, its cheap fares were offsetting its slower, noisier, snugger planes. At first both Aloha and Hawaiian Air balked at matching Mid Pacific's lower fares. "That was a mistake," says Bert Thomas. "That gave them a head start. Maybe we just hoped they would go away at first. But when they had grabbed a share of the market we realized we had to match them." Neither Aloha nor Hawaiian had the profit margins to do that and still make money.

What was so punishing was the duration of the battle with Mid Pacific, whose share of market gradually grew to nearly 20 percent. With both the visitor market and economy turned soft, little if any of the third airline's business represented new revenues. Mid Pacific's revenues came at the other carriers' expense.

Aloha's share of market slid to a low of 32 percent—down from 43 percent before Mid Pacific's arrival. In 1982 Aloha reported a net loss for the first time since the dark days before 1972. By then, Aloha had 10 Boeing 737s in service and, with

Joseph O'Gorman led the 1984 Aloha Pacific venture, and much more.

fuel costs soaring, it was costing a fortune to keep the planes in the air. The company couldn't boost revenues in the soft economy, so it had to trim costs wherever it could.

President Ed Swofford took a 20 percent pay cut to help lighten expenses. Other executives took 10 percent cuts. Aloha's union members were asked for concessions. One union, the International Association of Machinists, almost walked off the job, but decided against it at the last minute.

Though it never came to an open break with employees, the concessions forced on the Machinists and others signaled that the familiar 'ohana atmosphere that pervaded Aloha in its early years had evolved into a more formal, traditional management/employee relationship. Times had changed dramatically in the airline industry, and in Hawaii.

Despite its growth pains, Aloha received fewer customer complaints that year than any other airline in the country—another tradition in the making.

Swofford's contract with Aloha expired in 1983, and, being nearly 65, he wanted to retire. To replace him, the company hired strapping, 39-year-old Joseph R. O'Gorman, an experienced executive from United Airlines.

Though his tenure as Aloha's president and CEO would last less than two years, many people credit O'Gorman's administration as being one of the most significant in the airline's history. They say it was he who positioned the company not only to weather the storm of deregulation, but to succeed in the turbulent years that followed.

"Joe knew the fast track; he knew what had to be done to compete in the new airline industry; and he, more than anybody, refocused the board's thinking and led the transition from the old days to the new," says Brenda F. Cutwright, who joined Aloha as its controller in 1984. But if refocusing Aloha on the future was O'Gorman's greatest contribution, it isn't what he is most remembered for.

Up to that point, Aloha had resisted all of deregulation's expansion and other temptations. But O'Gorman felt there was no way the company could grow without breaking out of its inter-island mold. And he felt growing was the only way to fly in the airline industry's wild, post-deregulation environment.

So Aloha leased a DC-10 from O'Gorman's alma mater, United Airlines, and launched a new route to Taipei, the capital of Taiwan. Under the banner "Aloha

Pacific," the plane flew twice weekly between Honolulu and Taipei, with a stop-over each way at Guam. The idea was to expand the route to Japan, but that would have to await the approval of Japanese authorities—often an uncertain, politically complicated matter.

Meantime, O'Gorman ordered another redo of Aloha's livery. Away went the "flower power" insignia and in came a simpler, bolder look: a stylized, bright orange "Aloha" on each plane's fuselage and tail.

Actually, Aloha's plunge into the Western Pacific was far less brazen than it looked. It was a trial run, executed with a minimum of cost. Cabin crews for the long Taipei route were borrowed from the company's inter-island flight personnel. So were most of the ground crews. Insofar as possible, everything was set up to permit a quick bail-out if the trial didn't pan out.

"I voted to try the new Pacific route," says Herbert C. Cornuelle, who had become an Aloha director in the '70s. He was one of the "outside" directors—those who were not also officers of the company. Others included the three IASCO directors, who weren't to leave for an-other year or so, Stuart Ho, banker John Bellinger—the same person who had given Aloha

Visitors board Aloha Pacific's DC-10 at the Taipei route inaugural.

its first bank loan 25 years earlier—and another old friend, Dave Benz, president of Tongg Publishing Co.

Cornuelle was one of the most respected executives in Hawaii. He had been president and CEO of Dillingham Corp., one of the state's largest companies until it went private and split up in the early 1980s. He then became a trustee of the Campbell Estate, one of Hawaii's major landowners. The lanky, soft-talking executive is admired for his conservative, pragmatic ways. But Aloha's new Pacific route was a justified gamble, in his estimation. "A company doesn't get anywhere if it doesn't take some chances," he says. "But you have to limit your risks."

In January, 1985, six months after Aloha Pacific began flying the Taipei route, the operation was shut down. Passenger demand hadn't lived up to expectations, perhaps in part because the Japan link hadn't materialized. A more significant factor, however, was the disappointment of Joe O'Gorman's plans for the Honolulu-Guam segment of the route. Pan Am had recently stopped service to Guam, and O'Gorman saw the vacuum as an opportunity for Aloha Pacific. Unfortunately, Continental Airlines, which was well-established in the market, saw the same opportunity and slashed its Guam fares by about one-third to ward off competitors. Without a feeder system like Continental's or any partnerships with other carriers that would help boost traffic on the new route, Aloha simply couldn't compete.

So the board decided to cut its losses—which, because of the cautious planning, weren't particularly severe. The company was able to realize a $3 million gain on the disposal of the DC-10 used for the Taipei route—wiping out half its total loss on the venture. A little bruised but much wiser, Aloha went back to doing what it did best, serving the inter-island market.

"One thing I like about Aloha Airlines is its ability to stay focused, to keep its eye on the ball," says Cornuelle. He credits Hung Wo Ching for a lot of that concentration. "Hung Wo was one of the few truly strategic thinkers I've ever known," says the veteran executive. "He saw beyond the horizon."

Aloha's pullback from overseas expansion may have been the decisive moment in its long rivalry with Hawaiian Airlines. While Aloha resisted any more deregulation temptations, Hawaiian did not. The older airline began service from Honolulu to several Mainland cities—in direct competition with giants like United—and even launched routes into the South Pacific. For equipment it used some leased L-1011s, a wide-bodied, three-engined jet that manufacturer Lockheed was phasing out of production. Hawaiian Air also started an international charter service, using some elderly Boeing 707s. The result gave the airline not only a sprawling network of facilities to staff and service, but a menagerie of aircraft to fly and maintain.

"The turning point between Aloha and Hawaiian came when Hawaiian decided to fly overseas," says Aloha director Stuart Ho. "For Hawaiian it was a devastating decision. It led directly to their loss of leadership in the inter-island market."

Regarding Aloha's brief overseas venture, Ho says, "We didn't hesitate to get out when we saw it was a miscalculation." The decision was the primary cause of a $1.9 million loss for Aloha in 1984, but that was the extent of the damage.

But O'Gorman's chief contributions to Aloha's future were less dramatic than the Taipei route—and far more lasting. He ordered a series of customer surveys that

Maury Myers: Flying on time counts most.

produced some important market intelligence that the company put to good use. One finding pointed to the importance of on-time performance and O'Gorman made schedule reliability a permanent cornerstone of the company. Punctuality in all matters, from plane departures to company meetings, became a way of life at the airline.

Another innovation suggested by the surveys was creation of a first class section on Aloha's inter-island flights. That idea was also implemented, it was an immediate success, and became a permanent feature.

A third change that was tried and then quickly abandoned was seat assignments. "They didn't work," says A. Maurice Myers, a former Continental Airlines executive who O'Gorman hired to head Aloha's marketing operations. "Our flights were too short, too frequent, and too full to bother with seat assignments. It created confusion and when that started delaying our flights, we dropped seat assignments like a hot potato. The surveys showed that if you didn't fly on time there was nothing else—nothing—you could do to please the customers," recalls Myers.

So on-time performance got top priority, a spot it has held ever since.

O'Gorman also made a deal with his old company, United Airlines, that extended the giant carrier's frequent flier program—"Mileage Plus"—to flights on Aloha. That and other arrangements made with United gave Aloha improved access to the armies of passengers United flies to the Islands, something that soon emerged as a key advantage in the fiercely competitive inter-island market.

And on that score, O'Gorman quickly arrived at a strategy for meeting upstart competitors like Mid Pacific Airlines. With the backing of Chairman Hung Wo Ching and other directors, O'Gorman decided the only way to meet the cut-rate competition was head-on. Aloha matched Mid Pacific's low inter-island fares selectively, based on aircraft capacity. It enabled the company to offer the same fares on the same number of seats as Mid Pacific, but not across the board, allowing Aloha to partially avoid the operating losses caused by the steep discounts.

Aloha helped develop this so-called "controlled capacity" discounting system, which has since been used by many other airlines across the country. At the same time, in its marketing Aloha pushed its advantages over the cut-rate carrier—pluses such as its all-jet fleet (Mid Pacific flew propjets), its better service (Mid Pac's service was admittedly "bare bones"), and, perhaps most important, Aloha's growing reputation for on-time performance.

And O'Gorman did whatever else he could to even the odds. Mid Pacific began operations out of Honolulu International Airport's central terminal, which also serves all of the airport's overseas flights. Aloha and Hawaiian operated out of the airport's old inter-island terminal. Its main terminal location gave Mid Pac a clear advantage in serving inter-island passengers connecting with overseas flights. So O'Gorman helped get airport authorities to reassign Mid Pacific to the inter-island terminal, canceling its competitive edge.

"Mid Pacific had the same advantages that other new airlines had after deregulation of the industry," says O'Gorman. "Because of the aircraft they flew, their non-union workers and a lot of other minimum-cost features, they could operate much cheaper than an established carrier like Aloha. The industry was trying to find out what to do with these new deregulation carriers—how to compete with them. We knew we had to innovate, cut our costs and scramble," he says.

By reorganizing Aloha's management, O'Gorman cut about 30 percent from former operating costs in that area. "We had to streamline, and get new talent where we needed it most," he says.

Today, more than a decade later, those who were with the company then remember the whirlwind of changes brought by Joe O'Gorman. And O'Gorman remembers the times, too. "That was a very challenging period," he says. "We made a lot of changes in a short time. We had to. The industry had changed completely. But it wouldn't have happened, we couldn't have made it, if the employees—everybody—hadn't supported the change. With their help, we turned the company around. They were fantastic. I'll never forget them."

Joe O'Gorman left Aloha in May 1985 to become president of Denver-based Frontier Airlines. When that company became one of the many casualties of deregulation he returned to United Airlines, where he is now its executive vice

Aloha's 737 "QCs" in action in the late '80s: Double-duty was the answer.

president for operations.

O'Gorman was replaced at Aloha by his marketing chief, A. Maurice Myers—"Maury" to all those who know him. Myers was another product of the airline industry's fast track and wasted no time in picking up where O'Gorman left off.

One of the first things the energetic, personable Myers did was to make the next Boeing 737s acquired for Aloha's fleet special "QC" models. The "QC" stood for "Quick Change." The planes were fitted with extra-large doors to facilitate cargo loading, and their passenger seats were mounted on tracks that allowed their fast removal, enabling the plane to be converted easily from passenger to cargo configuration. The QCs were to do double duty, flying passengers during the day and cargo at night between Honolulu International Airport and the neighbor islands.

Before Aloha's introduction of modern jet cargo transport, inter-island air cargo service was largely provided by old propeller-driven planes and was often slow and unreliable. Earlier attempts to provide jet service had failed because they relied on cargo revenues alone and those couldn't meet the jets' higher capital and operating costs. Myers' solution of using the dual-purpose QC jets, combining passenger and cargo revenues to cover costs, worked beautifully.

Before long, Aloha was carrying most of the state's inter-island air cargo. It also stepped up the contract maintenance service it had performed for years for other airlines—mostly transient flights stopping off in Honolulu. With Aloha once again concentrating its operations in Hawaii, Myers looked for growth in diversifying the company's aviation services, and by building quality and reliability still further.

At the end of 1985, Aloha owned eight and leased seven Boeing 737s. Eight of the total were used in its inter-island operations and the remaining seven were leased to other airlines. When it could, the company took advantage of favorable financing and aircraft market conditions to acquire its planes, preferring to own them when the conditions were right. It was a policy begun by Ed Swofford and continued by O'Gorman and Myers. And it had built substantial assets on the company's books. By 1985, the aircraft were valued at about $180 million, against which there were debts of just $46 million—giving Aloha substantial equity in its planes.

Thanks in part to all the company stock that was sold during its early years, Aloha had thousands of local shareholders. Over the years, the company's stock, which was listed on the American Stock Exchange, had turned in a solid, though unspectacular performance. The market price hovered for years around $5 or $6 a share. Even during the IASCO episode, the price remained well under $10.

Suddenly, in the third quarter of 1985 the price turned sharply upward, approaching $10 a share. Still, management reasoned that wasn't unusual considering Aloha's recent earnings and the value of its stockholders' equity—which alone was worth $10. It was just that, not counting IASCO, there had never been much speculative interest in the company that might account for the sudden price rise. But that record, along with the country's financial markets, was changing.

Uniforms Over the Years

1948

1950

1959

1965

1962

1969

50 Years of Aloha

1973

1976

1979   **1983**

1986

1989

1993

An Aloha 737 off Waikiki, in the late '80s. The airline's performance attracted attention on the Mainland.

Chapter 7: Keeping the Faith

A familiar battle cry in corporate boardrooms in the mid-1980s was "increasing shareholder value."

The market performance of a company's stock is traditionally affected much more by its profits than by its assets. It's less likely today, but before the corporate slenderizing of the late 1980s and early '90s some companies had huge assets that produced little income but added enormous wealth to their balance sheets. As a result, these companies were worth more dead, with their assets disposed of, than alive with the assets producing meager returns.

"Increasing shareholder value" was an attempt to shift more of the dormant, passive value of a company's assets into the active, negotiable value of its stock. A variety of methods were tried, but none was particularly successful and the market continued to prize earnings far more than assets. In the end, most companies just trimmed or encumbered their assets to make them less tempting.

The reason for the furor was the emergence of the corporate raider. By the mid-'80s, bands of enterprising investors, often with little more to their names than a good credit rating, were roving the business landscape on the lookout for companies whose stock was priced well beneath their asset value. Typically using borrowed money, a "raider" would buy chunks of a targeted stock on the open market at the undervalued price. The buying would drive up the stock's value.

Then the raider would announce his intention to buy control of the company, triggering another wave of buying.

The raider then had a choice: Carry out the buyout or sell the shares he had accumulated, typically for a lot more than he paid for them. Either choice could produce a killing.

The decision often depended on how the victim's management reacted to the threat, and the depth of the raider's pockets.

The raider would offer to buy all or most of the company shares he didn't already own at a certain price. If management didn't like the price, or for some other reason rejected the offer, the raider could launch a "hostile takeover." This involved a "tender offer"—an offer to buy the stock made directly to individual shareholders. If enough shares were tendered, the raider won control of the company.

Then the real beauty of a hostile takeover might emerge. Assuming the raider got the stock at a good price, and the company's assets were indeed worth much more than the stock's value reflected, the victim could end up paying for its own takeover.

The raider would borrow the money used to buy out the other stockholders and when the purchase was completed and he had control of the company he would sell off enough of its assets to pay off his loan. He would be left debt-free to do as he pleased with what was left of the company.

But a raider didn't have to go that far to make a lot of money. He could simply get the victim to buy him off. It was usually considered worth payment of a considerable premium just to get rid of a raider. If he bought the stock at a good price, and had driven up its value considerably, getting the current market price plus an attractive premium could bring a hefty profit with relatively little effort. This ploy became known as "greenmail."

As they eyed the world outside Hawaii, Aloha Airline's directors, especially those who owned a big stake in the company, worried about the investor interest it was attracting. They hired investment bankers Bear, Stearns & Co. to recommend ways to build shareholder value. But before a strategy could be developed,

Sheridan Ing: Local owners are more sensitive.

Aloha's stock price again began to climb. It soon passed $10 and reached $11 a share.

On a Friday in January, 1986, the American Stock Exchange suspended trading on Aloha's shares—a routine practice when trading volume was unusually heavy. By then, the share price was $13.50.

When trading re-opened the following Monday, the stock jumped to $17.50 a share. This time, the directors knew more of the reason. Chairman Hung Wo Ching and a long-time shareholder and board Vice Chairman Sheridan C.F. Ing agreed to pool their holdings in the company with other key owners in the event of a hostile takeover attempt.

All together, the group controlled 38 percent of Aloha's common shares and 51 percent of its preferred. The market was reacting to the fact that major owners Ching and Ing had decided to circle the wagons.

"Sherry was very concerned about keeping control of Aloha Airlines in Hawaii," says Sheridan Ing's widow, Julia Ing. "He strongly believed that local owners would be more sensitive to the workers' needs, the broader needs of the community, and the best interests of the state's economy. Those were the main reasons for keeping local companies in local hands."

But by the end of the month, the company's share price topped $20 and the heavy buying continued. Then Maury Myers got a phone call from Dallas. On the line was a young man who identified himself as Norman Seigal. He said that he and two partners had acquired 16 percent of Aloha's stock and that the trio, calling themselves CNS Partners, would like a meeting with Aloha's directors to discuss buying the company.

CNS's purchases hadn't been solely responsible for the runup in Aloha's stock price. The partners were, in fact, latecomers in the buying and had an average purchase price of about $20 a share. Buying them off, if it came to that, could be expensive.

Then CNS sent Aloha an offer. The partners said they were interested in acquiring the 84 percent of Aloha's common shares they didn't already own. They offered a price of $27.50 a share. The stock was at the time trading for about $24.

Speaking for their owner group, Hung Wo Ching and Sheridan Ing rejected the offer. They cited their desire to keep the airline's control local. They noted that the company's rules required that a majority of both the common and preferred shareholders approve any merger. And they controlled a slim majority of the preferred stock votes.

Aloha's leaders considered the CNS bid a typical case of corporate raiding. They determined that the money used to buy the 16 percent of Aloha's stock was borrowed. They concluded that the $46 million required to buy the rest of the stock at $27.50 a share would also be borrowed—this time counting on getting control of Aloha's substantial assets. The raiders could easily finance their buyout, once they had gained control, by selling some of Aloha's 737s.

But that would have ruined 40 years of hard work, sacrifice and dreams. And Ching and his associates weren't about to do that, even though they would have personally profited greatly from the sale of their shares at the offer price.

The CNS partners continued for a time to press their bid, increasing their holdings to more than 20 percent. At Aloha's 1986 annual shareholders meeting, the partners appeared in person to plead their case. They rented a conference room down the hall from the hotel annual meeting site and wooed curious stockholders with punch and *pupus*.

But to no avail. At the end of 1986 Aloha's major owners bought back CNS's stock at a price of $25.50 a share, plus $2 a share to defray costs. All together, the raiders got just what they had offered Aloha's other stockholders. But by this time, with all the costs involved in waging a year-long battle for control, the partners probably did no more than break even.

The expense, disruption and stress of fighting off the takeover attempt—the second such experience counting the earlier IASCO affair—led Aloha's major owners to a monumental decision. They decided to save the company from any more takeover trials by taking its stock off the public market. "Going private," as the move is called, involved buying all the Aloha stock not already in the owners' hands.

Not everybody agreed with the decision, even among Aloha's directors, but the company and its financial advisers proceeded with plans for the "LBO," which stands for "leveraged buyout"—another popular tactic then sweeping the country.

In an LBO, a company's insiders—usually senior executives—join forces to buy control of the company. They typically use the sort of "leveraging" employed by corporate raiders, borrowing against company assets, to finance the buyout. The big difference is that, far from hoping to turn a quick profit from selling company assets, LBO participants normally want to use the assets to build the company. Unlike raiders, they invest for the long haul.

Such was the case at Aloha Airlines. Its LBO was plainly motivated by the desire of owners Hung Wo Ching, Sheridan Ing and others both to keep Aloha flying and to keep its ownership in local hands. Hawaii control had been a cardinal rule throughout the company's history. "With so much uncertainty in the air, Sherry thought that need existed more than ever," says Julia Ing.

Operationally, Aloha was in great shape, despite all the distractions. The year 1986 was producing a bumper crop of passengers and other business. In May the company formed a new cargo sales and services department to handle the rapid growth of its inter-island air freight business. It added two more 737s that upped its fleet to 10. It was flying 147 daily flights with 25 percent more seats than just a year before. And once again Aloha registered the fewest passenger complaints of any scheduled airline in the country. It even started 737 charter service for Air Tungaru to the mid-Pacific Republic of Kiribati—a milestone route for twin-engine jets.

Hawaii's visitor industry had finally recovered from the 1981-82 recession. In 1986 the state's visitor count climbed to 5.6 million, up 15 percent from the year before. Aloha added two more 737s, bringing its fleet to 12. In one year, its passenger capacity had increased 50 percent.

In November, the stockholder group led by Hung Wo Ching and Sheridan Ing

An Island Air commuter: Filling the gaps in statewide service.

reached agreement for the purchase of all the company's outstanding stock. The terms had been worked out by "outside" directors Herbert Cornuelle and Stuart Ho, with the help of a team of specialists hired to assist them.

Both Cornuelle and Ho recall their work vividly. "We were extremely careful in how we valued the stock," says Cornuelle. "We wanted to be fair to everybody."

Though there had been misgivings among some owners, many of whom had owned shares since Aloha's earliest days, there were no serious objections to the terms of the buyout. All shareholders not participating in the LBO were to receive $28.50 per share for their stock, which was a dollar more than the greenmail price paid to CNS Partners. That put the total cost to the buyers at $58 million. Co-LBO leader Sherry Ing was instrumental in arranging the buyout, and for his role was made chairman of the new board of directors, with Hung Wo Ching becoming vice chairman.

The company's shareholders approved the terms and the buyout was completed early in 1987. Aloha Airlines became privately, and locally, owned.

At about that time the company announced record 1986 operating earnings and revenues. President Maury Myers attributed the performance to the airline's dedication to quality service. A surging visitor market helped, too. And Japanese investors, loaded with cash and freer than ever to spend it as they wished, were arriving in Hawaii by the planeload.

Aloha again expanded in the only way it wanted to expand. Management had formed a holding company for the airline, called Aloha Airgroup, Inc., and through it acquired Princeville Airlines, a propjet commuter service that flew to Hawaii's small airfields that Aloha couldn't reach with its jets. The commuter's name was later changed to Aloha Island Air, and, eventually, with its propjet fleet expanded and modernized, simply to Island Air. The commuter airline operates as an independent sister company of Aloha Airlines under Aloha Airgroup, Inc.

Part of maximizing Aloha's return from the inter-island market was finding new ways to please passengers. Marketing whiz Maury Myers launched a variety of crowd-pleasers in the mid-'80s. Aloha had started its own frequent-flier awards system, the AlohaPass, in 1983 and in 1985 Myers added the Executive Club, which gave members extra benefits like express reservation service, a private lounge and early boarding privileges, and later the Alii Club, offering even more perks. In 1993, as a special attraction of Honolulu International Airport's elegant new Inter-Island Terminal, Aloha introduced a revolutionary Drive-Through Check-in gate for customers using the terminal's parking area.

Chapter 8:
"The Best We Can Possibly Be"

*O*nce it had gone private, Aloha was truly on its own. One of the advantages of public ownership is that it usually makes raising money—debt as well as equity financing—relatively easy. Going private limited Aloha's financing options. And running an airline requires frequent financing.

But Aloha was changing more than its financial structure. The mid-'80s brought a reassessment of what kind of airline Aloha wanted to be. The catalyst for this corporate soul-searching was the company's CEO, Maury Myers.

"We had reached a point where we had to make some basic decisions," Myers remembers. "We weren't sure about the economic future of our market, but we knew it was changing, and we knew we were changing, too. We felt we were on the threshold of something big."

Though the company could only sense it then, Aloha had begun a period of uninterrupted growth that would catapult it to the top of the inter-island market. In the mid-'80s, management could only guess what was ahead. Joe O'Gorman had begun raising the questions, and Myers continued.

He took key managers to the Big Island for some strategy sessions. The main question, Myers recounts, was, "What did we want Aloha to be?" The answer: "We wanted to be a world-class airline in the inter-island market." He defines "world class" as "being the best we can possibly be."

Hawaiian Air still had about 60 percent of the inter-island market and Aloha had the rest. Upstart Mid Pacific Airlines had run out of cash and shut down. But the market was changing. Myers needed to chart a course for the rest of the '80s and beyond.

One thing he did was to raise Aloha's profile in its home market. Employees were encouraged to become active in community affairs. Myers himself plunged into a number of outside activities. He became chairman of the Hawaii Visitors Bureau and spoke out on business and community issues. He was an early advocate of the visitor industry giving greater emphasis to Hawaii's unique history and cultural heritage as a means of distinguishing the Islands among a growing

New 737-400s on Boeing's assemblyline: Aloha took delivery of two, but times changed.

sea of competing tourist destinations.

Mid Pacific Airline's departure seemed to prove what people at both Aloha and Hawaiian had maintained all along about the size of their market. "This is a two-carrier market, and that's all there is to it," says the veteran Ed Swofford.

But Mid Pacific's experience wasn't to discourage others from trying, though they may not have disagreed with Swofford's assessment. For, as the '80s wore on, the life expectancy of one of Hawaii's established inter-island airlines grew uncertain. And it wasn't Aloha Airlines.

Aloha continued in an expansion mode, adding and replacing planes as aircraft availability, financing and market conditions warranted. It kept testing the market with more planes—pushing the envelope.

In mid-1988 came a blizzard of financial transactions. Included was the sale or sale and leaseback of eight 737-200s—the second model in the popular 737 series—the purchase and financing of a pair of new 737-300s, the payoff of some old aircraft loans, and a complicated sale of tax benefits. One purpose of the transactions was to streamline the company's balance sheet and help cash flow. But another was to modernize its fleet. For the flurry of financings followed one of the most dramatic events in aviation history.

On April 28, 1988, early in the afternoon of a typically sunny island day, Aloha Flight 243 took off from Hilo bound for Honolulu. A few minutes into the 30-minute flight, as the plane climbed through the 20,000-foot level over the Alenuihaha Channel, a huge section of the 737's fuselage just aft of the cockpit suddenly blew away. For 18 feet nothing remained of the fuselage above the cabin floor, leaving a half-dozen rows of passengers fully exposed, like in some bizarre cutaway drawing, to the open sky and raging winds. The roofless plane presented a scene that no one who saw it, however far removed, would ever forget.

For 13 agonizing minutes, Captain Robert "Bob" Schornstheimer and First Officer Mimi Tompkins struggled to keep the crippled 737 aloft as they headed for the nearest airfield. To the amazement of a world soon electrified by news accounts of the incident, Flight 243 landed safely at Kahului Airport on Maui. Though many passengers were injured by the fierce wind and flying debris, one of the miracles that day was that there was only one fatality. It was veteran flight attendant "C.B." Lansing.

When pilots Schornstheimer and Tompkins later visited Washington, then U.S. Representative Pat Saiki introduced a congressional resolution commending them for their heroism and skill aboard Flight 243. "I remember Clarabelle—'C.B.'," says Saiki. "I helped train her."

The Flight 243 incident launched a complete reassessment by the airline industry of the "aging aircraft" issue. An investigation determined that metal fatigue in the superstructure of the 737—undetectable by prescribed maintenance and inspection procedures at the time—had probably caused the rupture in the aircraft's "skin." The sudden release of cabin pressure had done the rest in blowing away the huge section of fuselage.

The number of cycles flown by a plane—the times it pressurizes and depressurizes in flight—became a major factor in assessing its safety. New testing procedures were developed for plane manufacturers, new inspection standards for industry regulators, new maintenance methods for operators. The whole airline industry, worldwide, was affected by Flight 243.

And for Aloha Airlines, it was a turning point. The company made some major changes after the incident.

The airline sold its four oldest basic model 737-200s, one of which was

Flight 243 crew members (l. to r.) Flight Attendant Jane Sato-Tomita, Captain Robert Schornstheimer, Flight Attendant Michelle Honda and First Officer Mimi Tompkins receive awards for heroism from U.S. Transportation Secretary Samuel K. Skinner.

involved in the Flight 243 incident. It acquired newer planes—either right off the Boeing assembly line or used, with a low number of cycles. Its in-service fleet grew to 18, despite a disturbing slowdown in the visitor market.

The visitor weakness came from economic troubles in both of Hawaii's largest tourist markets, the continental U.S. and Japan. The end of the Cold War was contributing to a severe recession on the Mainland—notably in California, Hawaii's biggest visitor source. But by 1990, with annual visitor arrivals approaching 7 million, state planners hoped they had the antidote to Mainland recessions.

Hawaii had become the favorite overseas destination of high-spending Japanese tourists, who were traveling abroad in ever-greater numbers. And Japan's post-war economy had so far proved recession-proof. Hawaii's leaders thought the Japanese would make up for any slump in travel from the Mainland.

After all, they reasoned, by 1990 Japan had a special stake in the Islands. In the late '80s there had been an unprecedented wave of Japanese investments in foreign real estate. Most went to the U.S., and tiny Hawaii was a favorite target, attracting nearly as much investment as commercial giants California and New York. The Japanese money fed a binge of new resort construction, particularly on the state's "neighbor islands."

But then Japan's "bubble economy" sprang a leak and the gusher of investments abruptly slowed. Japanese tourists, which accounted for nearly a quarter of Hawaii's total, continued to arrive, but they were a different breed than those of the '80s. They spent less and stayed for shorter periods.

The Persian Gulf War of early 1991 actually kept many Japanese travelers at home for a time. Simultaneously, Hawaii's westbound tourist market—largely from the Mainland—also shriveled. A deep recession gripped both the continental U.S. and Japan. The state's visitor industry, already worried about filling its new resorts, didn't know where to look for its 7 millionth customer. Tourism sputtered, stalled and headed into a three-year nose-dive—unprecedented until then. And Hawaii's whole economy swooned in sympathy.

Worldwide, it was also a terrible time for airlines, as troubled economies translated into fewer passengers. In the period 1990-92, the industry's accumulated losses reached a staggering $10 billion.

Amazingly, the industry bloodletting didn't greatly affect Aloha Airlines. Part of the reason was the company's culture of what Maury Myers calls "controlled frugality." The company had spent so many years pinching pennies that it seemingly couldn't overspend, at least on routine costs. Some people argued that too much was being spent on refleeting—buying new 737s that then cost upwards of $25 million apiece—but nobody could fault the company's controls on operating expenses. Myers says that many employees, in fact, had to be taught *not* to cut expenses too sharply. "They had to learn that it was okay to spend on some things," he recalls.

With costs contained, operating results were showing encouraging gains. The inter-island air cargo operation started in the '80s was doing well. By 1992 Aloha handled close to 90 percent of all intrastate air shipments.

But the biggest reason for the continued strength in earnings was what had happened to Aloha's share of the inter-island passenger market. Though tourism had turned soft, the company was now getting 60 percent of the market—up hugely from its traditional 30 to 40 percent. After years of playing second fiddle, Aloha had suddenly become Hawaii's largest inter-island airline.

Along with Aloha's new role came a new look. Gone were the orange and red colors dating back to the "Flower Power" designs of 20 years before. In their place were rich navy and guava colors decorating the 737s outside and in. But everything wasn't new. A stylish bird of paradise design—a company trademark since the days of the DC-3s—emblazoned the tails of all the planes. It symbolized both Aloha's tradition and its bright new future.

Briefly during this period another would-be third inter-island carrier emerged But the newcomer, Discovery Airways, quickly ran afoul of federal foreign ownership restrictions and never really got started.

The biggest contributor to Aloha's stunning market gain was its arch-rival, Hawaiian Air. In the mid-'80s Hawaiian began a series of financially disastrous years, largely the result of losses in its overseas routes. In 1992, it reported a $111 million deficit, a fearsome figure for any Hawaii company.

As Hawaiian battled its financial problems, its inter-island service deteriorated and it lost market share. The company sought protection under Chapter 11 of the federal bankruptcy laws, emerged in 1994, but continued to struggle. It abandoned some of its overseas routes, trimmed others, and made efforts to consolidate its fleet. But the long malaise left Aloha firmly in command of the inter-island market—the only market it ever really cared about.

But by late 1992 Aloha was also feeling the effects of the slump in tourism and Hawaii's faltering economy. And the extra costs involved in expanding its fleet gnawed at its operating margins. Even so, the year was headed for a modest profit when a force even more unpredictable than world economies knocked the whole state of Hawaii for a loop. It was a Force 5 hurricane called Iniki.

Hurricane Iniki damage on Kauai: Kicking the economy while it was down. Photo © 1992 Nikolas Konstantinou/Photo Resource Hawaii.

Before Iniki slammed into the island of Kauai on September 11, 1992, that market provided about 25 percent of Aloha's business. In a few hours of raging winds and crashing waves Kauai's economy was demolished and with it, temporarily, most of Aloha's business there. For the company, the natural disaster turned what otherwise would have been a modest profit for 1992 into a loss, ending a seven-year string of uninterrupted profits.

Chapter 9: Hawaii's Airline

Early in 1992 Aloha's management laid plans to take the company's stock public. After five years of private ownership, the company's owners—led by the Hung Wo Ching and Sheridan Ing families—felt it was time to earn a return on their long investments. But, primarily, Aloha needed the added financial flexibility public ownership would bring.

At the time, so-called "IPOs"—short for "initial public offerings"—were coming out in increasing numbers, as the stock market, weary of the dreary financial news emerging from the country's slumping economy, looked for new excitement. But the stock market is notoriously fickle. "Timing is very important," says J.W.A. "Doc" Buyers, chairman of C. Brewer & Co., the oldest of Hawaii's "Big Five" companies. Buyers was a close friend and confidante of Sherry Ing and the two frequently discussed the stock market. Brewer did an IPO with a subsidiary housing development company, called Brewer Homes, with gratifying results. So did another Honolulu-based developer, Schuler Homes.

Aloha planned its stock offering for June, 1992. But when June arrived, the market seemed sated with IPOs and the offering was postponed. It was rescheduled for July 1993, but as that date approached doubts rose that, because of the economic slowdown in Hawaii, Aloha might not be able to deliver immediately the strong earnings Wall Street investors expected. So the offering was again delayed, this time indefinitely. "Market investors had become very finicky," says Doc Buyers.

Aloha was eyeing its future conservatively. With its new market dominance, any improvement in the Hawaii economy and its big tourist industry would benefit the airline. Hurricane Iniki had been an aberration that, in effect, kicked the Hawaii economy when it was already down. Yet it had taken the hurricane to push Aloha into the loss column in 1992. Before that, Aloha had racked up seven straight years of profits, and in 1991 had a robust $8 million profit before an accounting change trimmed that in half.

The airline soon demonstrated its good health by bouncing right back from the '92 loss, despite its still-sluggish market. The double blow dealt the Hawaii economy by the simultaneous decline of its two largest tourist markets—the continental U.S. and Japan—would take more time to heal. But Aloha was back in the black by 1993, still registering the fewest complaints of any airline, and growing again despite the conditions around it. The growth came largely from the continued decline of the company's lifelong rival, Hawaiian Air.

What's more, in searching for the capital to keep it flying, Hawaiian eventually lost its local ownership, leaving Aloha the only Hawaii carrier still in Island hands. Another new carrier appeared on the inter-island market, this one called Mahalo Air, but its ownership ties reach beyond Hawaii.

Late in 1993, Maury Myers decided his work at Aloha was finished and resigned to accept the presidency of Phoenix-based America West Airlines. His departure was scheduled for early 1994.

Before Myers left, the company and the Honolulu business community were saddened by the death of Sheridan "Sherry" Ing. The mild-mannered but razor-sharp businessman, who had been chairman of Aloha since it went private in 1987, succumbed after a long bout with cancer. He was replaced as chairman by Han H. "Sonny" Ching, who had been co-vice chairman with his father, Hung Wo Ching.

In addition, Sherry Ing's son, local businessman Richard K.M. Ing, and David A. Heenan, then president of Theo. H. Davies & Co., were elected to the board. Heenan has since become a trustee of the Honolulu-based Campbell Estate.

Chairman Sonny Ching: Keeping the old commitment alive.

Myers was succeeded as president on an interim basis by Thomas F. Derieg, who had been Aloha's senior vice president of operations. In May, 1994, after an extensive search, the company hired Glenn R. Zander, a veteran executive from Trans World Airways, as Myers' permanent successor.

If it was Maury Myers' marketing background that prompted his efforts to sharpen the airline's customer service and on-time performance, it was his successor Glenn Zander's financial experience with mega-carrier TWA that brought a new and sharper focus to the company's operations. By streamlining here and tightening there, Zander has put Aloha, from its balance sheet to its fleet, in fighting trim.

An Aloha 737 in 1990s livery.

50 Years of Aloha

Chapter 10:
Positioned for the Long Haul

*T*he change in leadership emphasis came at a good time. Upstart Mahalo Air continued to chip away at the market share of the two established carriers, Aloha and Hawaiian Air. Hawaiian emerged from its bankruptcy protection in September 1994 determined to recapture the market lead it had lost. Over the next 18 months Hawaiian cut its workforce, won wage concessions from its unions, and got a New York investment group led by Smith Management Co. to sink $20 million into its sputtering operations. In exchange, Hawaiian gave the New Yorkers controlling interest in the company.

CEO Glenn Zander: Fine tuning is producing big benefits.

Under Zander, Aloha launched several changes in the way it operated, the way it was financed, the way it appeared to customers, even in the way it looked at itself. All the changes were designed to increase performance and profitability. Zander calls the changes "positioning the company for the long haul."

In 1995, Zander reorganized Aloha's management team to add strength to those areas where it was most needed. He brought in new senior managers in marketing and operations and created a senior management auditing position to focus on staffing, inventory and revenue management.

But easily the most significant of the changes Zander made was standardization of Aloha's aircraft fleet. That means more than flying all Boeing 737s—something the airline has done since the early '70s. Zander honed standardization still further to using only the same series of 737s.

In the late 1980s and beginning of the '90s, Hawaii's tourism was growing by leaps and bounds and Aloha geared up for the heavier passenger loads by acquiring larger capacity planes. These were the Boeing 737-300 and 737-400 models.

They cost more and were more expensive to fly and maintain than the 737-200s Aloha had used until then, but they had more room for the anticipated continued rise in passengers.

When, instead, tourism and the economy plunged in 1992 and beyond, Aloha found the larger-model 737s inefficient in the suddenly changed marketplace. So the company once again refleeted, switching to advanced models of the more economical 737-200s. In 1995, Aloha subleased two of its 737-300 planes and sold two 737-400 models, as well as two 737-300s then on lease to another carrier.

Aloha Airlines' 50 Years of Growth

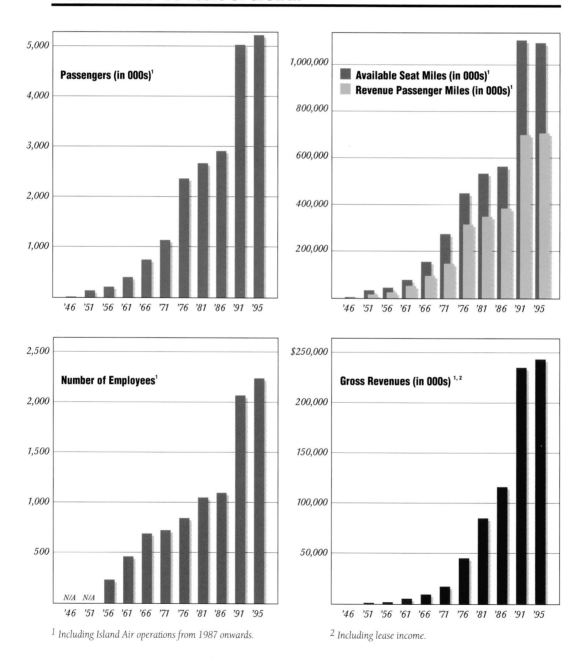

1 Including Island Air operations from 1987 onwards.   2 Including lease income.

The 737-200s that replaced these planes were leased, rather than purchased, saving what otherwise would have been a huge cash outlay. At the same time, the passenger cabins of the 200s were reconfigured to add seats, in effect offsetting the seats lost with the disposal of the 300s and 400s. Explains Brenda Cutwright, Aloha's chief financial officer: "Standardizing our fleet and redesigning the planes so there is no loss of capacity cost us money up front, and that is reflected in our 1995 figures. But, having taken the financial hit, we're in excellent shape for 1996 and beyond."

The refleeting was completed in 1996, leaving Aloha with an all-Advanced 737-200 fleet. The economies realized by the 200s over the larger models in lower lease rents, parts inventory, maintenance costs and landing fees will produce an annual savings for Aloha of about $10 million—a gain that should drop straight to the company's bottom line, favorably affecting earnings for years to come.

Increasing the capacity of the 737-200s was accomplished by refitting the cabins with new "slim line" leather seats, a model that makes more efficient use of space and actually provides passengers with greater leg room and freedom of movement than earlier seats.

The new seats were part of a complete interior redecoration of the aircraft. The emphasis was on quality, from the stylish colors to the leather-upholstered seats. It's part of the value Aloha now endeavors to give its customers in every phase of its operations. With a fare structure that is highly competitive, both on a local and industrywide scale, the airline is determined, says President Zander, to deliver top value for the travel dollar.

That being the case, and with leaner, more efficient operations and a balance sheet clear of obstacles, Aloha is well positioned for whatever the future brings.

Glenn Zander, along with most of the economists and business leaders of Hawaii, feels that future is rapidly brightening. Zander sees steady growth ahead for tourism, which is the linchpin of the state's economy and accounts for the largest share of Aloha's passenger market.

The expectations are based largely on trends in the Japanese and other Asian markets. "Japan's market has lots of room for growth, and other Asian markets, such as Korea and Taiwan, are just opening up," says the Aloha president.

The Asian market, which continued to grow throughout Japan's recent economic problems, is already the biggest in the world, and for more than a decade the United States has done more business across the Pacific than with its traditional trading partners across the Atlantic.

Fueling the surge in eastbound traffic to Hawaii—visitors originating in Asia and the South Pacific—is the state's emergence as a premier "shopping center" for the entire Pacific Basin. Retail sales in the Islands have mushroomed, largely because of the boom in tourist shopping. The phenomenon has caught the attention of the world's largest and classiest retailers, triggering a swarm of new Island outlets in recent years.

On top of this, in 1998 Honolulu will open its long-awaited convention center, accessing as never before the giant meetings and conventions segment of the world tourism market. Both junketing shoppers and meeting-goers are gregarious travelers, promising what should be a wave of new inter-island passengers in the years ahead.

Zander's plans for Aloha cover more than growing sales and profits. He says the company wants to recapture the employee dedication that it enjoyed during the earlier years. "The company grew very suddenly in the late '80s," he says. "We hired a lot of new employees. Many of them don't know about the intense, almost personal commitment our people used to have. It's given us a kind of two-company culture—the old company and the new company," he says.

"We want to bring those two cultures into one, by retaining the strengths of each. It's a little like changing a tire while the car is still moving," Zander smiles.

Zander says management is still working on what Maury Myers called employees' "controlled frugality." "People have to learn that if they aren't spending money they shouldn't automatically assume it's the right thing to do." He says the aim is "maximizing the company's long-term profitability." Zander says that sometimes requires spending money to save money, such as in the recent refleeting program.

While Aloha's employee base has grown considerably in the last decade and relationships have become more structured, the changes of the early and mid-1980s produced some very positive results. There was a chain reaction of benefits. The employee sacrifices of the Swofford era made the company more competitive and set the stage for future growth. It created a win-win situation, as subsequent negotiations traded productivity gains for higher wages and benefits. All this helped position the company for the rapid growth that took it to the top of the inter-island market, and it made today's Aloha employees well compensated by industrywide standards.

It is a winning balance created in the '80s, nurtured in the early '90s, and it now may be Aloha's strongest asset in facing the future. For one of the few certainties that lie ahead is an increased demand for operating efficiency. That and another Aloha trademark: focus.

Brenda Cutwright calls the company's operating watchwords "F&F"—"flexible and focused." "We've got to be flexible enough to meet changing conditions, but focused on our objectives," she says. "We've seen what happens to an airline when that isn't the case. In the mid-1980s we had 38 percent of the inter-island market and Hawaiian Air had 62 percent. Today, the positions are reversed. F&F made the difference."

Zander says Aloha's new dominance of the inter-island market was the product of two things. "We were at the right place at the right time" when the long-time market leader Hawaiian Air faltered. "And we were focused on our niche in the market." Of the two factors, "being focused was the more crucial. It's what is going to keep us on top in the future."

In the first days of spring, 1996, as Aloha Airlines neared the celebration of its 50th anniversary, the company lost the man who taught it the value of being focused. Dr. Hung Wo Ching, the octogenarian to whom Aloha, and Hawaii, owes so much, died after a long illness. He served as the company's vice chairman until the end.

As Aloha Airlines celebrates its 50th anniversary, it is outwardly a far cry from the struggling TPA of the promise-filled early years. Yet, despite all the changes in the airline and the island market it serves, Aloha is still in many ways "The People's Airline," and true to the beliefs on which it was built.

Fundamental to those beliefs was an abiding confidence in Hawaii and its people—a special loyalty that runs deep through the culture of the Islands. David Heenan, the professional manager and former business school dean who now serves as an Aloha director, describes the commitment that he saw in company leaders Hung Wo Ching and Sheridan Ing.

"They had a special feeling toward the people who grew up here," says Heenan. "The company reflects that caring. You can still see it in many ways. And it's a rare and priceless thing."

The history of Aloha Airlines parallels the economic development of modern Hawaii. Each was a mirror image of the other, from the free-wheeling, gutsy days after World War II, to the heady growth that followed statehood, to the maturing years of the '70s and '80s, and the whirling events of the '90s, as Hawaii searched for its place in the looming 21st, the "Pacific Century."

So, too, are the futures of the Aloha State and Aloha Airlines entwined; and their hopes, dreams and expectations are much the same.

Aloha Airlines Milestones

DC-3, 1946

*July 26, 1946:
Trans-Pacific
Airlines'
inaugural flight.*

*1956: President
Eisenhower approves
TPA's permanent
certification.*

*1958: Dr. Hung Wo
Ching takes over
management,
changes TPA's name
to Aloha Airlines.*

*1963-1968: Aloha
continues to upgrade its
fleet with a succession of
newer, larger planes,
following the F-27 with
the Vickers Viscount and
the all-jet BAC-111.*

BAC 111, 1965

1946   1956   1966

*1949: President Truman
signs TPA's temporary
certification, permitting
scheduled flights.*

*1959: Hawaii
becomes the 50th state;
jet travel starts
between Hawaii and
the Mainland; Aloha
Airlines introduces the
Fairchild F-27 propjet
to replace its prop-
driven DC-3s.*

*1969: The year of the
Funbird. Boeing 737s
replace the BAC-111s
and Viscounts in Aloha's
fleet, introducing "The
Wonderful World of
Aloha."*

F-27, 1959

Vickers Viscount, 1963

50 Years of Aloha

1981: The first of a succession of new inter-island airlines, Mid Pacific, emerges; triggers costly fare wars.

Boeing 737-400, 1992

1984: Sister-carrier Aloha Pacific is formed, starts DC-10 service to Taipei.

1972: Lengthy merger negotiations with Hawaiian Airlines broken off, Aloha reports a banner year.

1986: Takeover attempt by Dallas-based CNS Partners. The bid is repulsed and Aloha's board decides to take the company private.

1987-1992: Aloha grows rapidly, the result of a surging tourist market and the steady decline of arch-rival Hawaiian Airlines. By 1992, despite a downturn in Hawaii's visitor arrivals, Aloha caps a seven-year run of increasing profits by emerging as the dominant airline in its market.

1976: California-based International Air Service Co. —IASCO—buys an interest in Aloha; announces intent to take control. The bid is refused, eventually repulsed.

1976

1986

1996

1978: Congress deregulates the U.S. airline industry.

1987: Leveraged buyout completed, led by long-time board members Hung Wo Ching and Sheridan Ing.

1985: Taipei service halted; Aloha refocuses on inter-island market with a new look, new planes, and diversification into new air cargo service.

Boeing 737-200, 1974

Boeing 737-300, 1986

Acknowledgements

The author wishes to thank all those Aloha Airlines employees, past and present, and the many others who contributed so freely of their time and memories to the writing of this book. Many are mentioned in its pages. But many are not. And to all is owed an equal debt of gratitude for helping tell this story, which is really their story. *Mahalo nui loa.*

Bill Wood

Index

A

Air Cargo 71
Air Cargo, Expansion of Aloha Service 56
Allen, Robert C. 18, 30
Aloha Airlines, Replaces TPA Name 33
Aloha Pacific Airlines 51, 52
Arab Oil Embargo 45
Asian Markets 79

B

BAC-111 38, 40
Bellinger, John D. 51
Bellinger, John D., Makes First Bank Loan to Company 33
Benz, David A 10, 11, 13, 15, 18, 24, 31, 33, 52
Big Five Companies 10, 73
Boeing 737 23, 24, 39, 42, 49, 50, 53, 54, 56, 61, 62, 63, 64, 70, 71, 77
Boeing 737 "QC" 56
Buyers, J.W.A. "Doc" 73

C

Char, Kenneth F.C. 43, 47
Ching, Dr. Hung Wo 1, 15, 16, 18, 21, 33, 36, 40, 42, 43, 45, 46, 52, 54, 62, 63, 64, 65, 73, 74, 81
Ching, Han H. "Sonny" 74
CNS Partners 63, 64, 65
Common Fare 44
Convention Center 79
Cordero, Raymond "Spike" 9
Cornuelle, Herbert C. 51, 65
Corporate Raiders 61
Cullen, George 11
Cutwright, Brenda F. 50, 78, 80

D

Deregulation, Airline Industry 47

Derieg, Thomas F. 75

Discovery Airways 71

Diversification, Aloha's Aviation Services 56

Dock Strike 1949 24

Douglas DC-3 7, 8, 9, 10, 18, 24, 26, 27, 30, 31, 33, 36, 38, 44, 71

Douglas DC-9 38

E

Economou, Peter 27

Eisenhower, Dwight D., Signs Permanent Certification 32

Entertainers, Employee Troupes 27

Entertainment, In-Flight 26

F

Fairchild F-27 36

Fairchild F-27, replaces DC-3s 33

Family Fare 30

Flight 243 68, 69

Flower Power 40, 51, 71

Fuel Price 49

Funbirds 40

G

Going Private 64

"Greenmail" 62, 65

Guam 51

H

Haole (Caucasian Establishment) 10, 11, 16

Hawaii Visitors Bureau (HVB) 18, 19, 30, 67

Hawaiian Airlines, Successor to Inter-Island Airlines 17, 19, 25, 30, 31, 33, 38, 42, 46, 52, 67, 74, 77

Heenan, David A. 74, 81

Ho, Chinn 45

Ho, Stuart T.K. 45, 51, 53, 65

Honolulu International Airport, Move From Lagoon Drive 25

Hui, Investment 15

Hurricane Iniki 72, 73

I

Imai, Helen 12, 13
Ing, Julia 62, 64
Ing, Richard K.M. 74
Ing, Sheridan C.F. 62, 63, 64, 65, 73, 74, 81
Initial Public Offering "IPO" 73
Inouye, Daniel K. 3, 16, 17
Inter-Island Airlines 21, 24, 25
Inter-Island Passenger Market, Share of 36, 49, 67, 71, 80
International Air Service Co. (IASCO) 46, 47, 51, 56, 57, 64
International Association of Machinists 50
Intrastate Air Shipments 71

J

Japan 51
Japanese, Investments 70
Japanese, Tourists 70
Jet Service, First Passenger Jets From West Coast 37
John Rodgers Field 7

K

Kagoshima, Ted 31
Kea, Baba 43
King, Richard "Dick" 18, 25, 26, 27, 30, 33, 43

L

Leveraged Buyout ("LBO") 64, 65
Load Factor 36, 44, 45
Lucas, Louis "Captain Luke" 7, 8, 9, 11, 27, 38, 39

M

MacGregor, Robert "Bob" 13, 18, 19, 25
Magoon, John 42
Mahalo Airlines 74, 77
McDermott, John 39, 43
Mergers, with Hawaiian Air 36, 42, 46
Mid Pacific Airlines 49, 67, 68
Mitsukoshi Building, TPA headquarters 12, 19
Myers, A. Maurice 53, 56, 63, 65, 67, 71, 74, 75

O

O'Gorman, Joseph R. 50, 53, 54
Olson, Al 7, 8, 11

P

Pacific Century 81
Pacific Route Awards 41
Pake (Chinese) Resident 11

R

Recession, Antidote 70
Recession, National 49, 64
Refleeting 71, 77

S

Saiki, Pat Fukuda 17, 27, 69
Scheduled Service, Application 21
Scheduled Service, Requirements 25
Seigal, Norman 63
Snyder, Malmorina Ricopuerto "Mellie" 12, 24, 26, 32, 36
Statehood, Hawaii Becomes 50th State 36
Swofford, Edward E. 47, 50, 56, 68

T

Taipei, Route 50, 52
The People's Airline 16
Thomas, Bert 43
Tongg, Ruddy 8, 10, 11, 12, 13, 17, 18, 24, 33
Tourism, Annual Visitor Count 19, 44, 45, 49, 70
TPA, Rivalry with Inter-Island Airlines 24
Trans-Pacific Airlines (TPA) 7, 8, 9, 10, 11, 12, 13, 15, 16, 17, 18, 19, 21, 24, 25, 26, 27, 30, 31, 32, 33
Truman, Harry S. 21, 24, 32

U

Umaki, Elsie 16, 31
Umaki, Roy 16

V

Vickers Viscount 38, 41, 43, 44
Volcano Flights 26

Y

Yamashiro, Sakai "Andy" 32

Z

Zander, Glenn R. 75 - 80